D1272024

THE SECRET OF TACTICAL CHESS

THE SECRET OF TACTICAL CHESS

FRED REINFELD
Introduction by Al Horowitz

COLLIER BOOKS
A Division of Macmillan Publishing Co., Inc.
NEW YORK
COLLIER MACMILLAN PUBLISHERS
LONDON

Macmillan Publishing Co., Inc.
866 Third Avenue, New York, N.Y. 10022
Collier-Macmillan Canada Ltd., Toronto, Ontario

The Secret of Tactical Chess was originally published in a hardcover edition by Thomas Y. Crowell Company and is reprinted by arrangement with the Fred Reinfeld Trust.

Library of Congress Catalog Card Number: 58-6612

First Collier Books Edition 1973

Second Printing 1974

Printed in the United States of America

Contents

Introduction

by Al Horowitz

If someone were to take a survey of chess masters, asking them what single characteristic they thought contributes most to success at the game, the more introspective among them would reply "alertness." Alertness on one level is that minimal attention required to be sure that you don't put your pieces on squares where your opponent can take them off, and of course to snap off your opponent's pieces should he afford you the opportunity to do so. On a somewhat loftier plane, it means the ability to take swift and inexorable advantage of your opponent's inaccuracies, no matter how small, and to play as accurately as possible yourself—the winner at chess is invariably the one who makes the fewer mistakes. At the end of a long tournament, whether it be the championship of a small-town club or a major international event, the winner is usually the player who has taken best advantage of his tactical opportunities.

Alertness, then, in this context, means alertness to tactics. In our chess daydreams we often see ourselves seated on a raised stage with a hushed audience attending at the same time to our every fidgit and a huge demonstration board behind us while we enmesh our hapless opponent in webs of subtlest strategy, but in real life it is our ability to see mate in two moves that keeps baby in new shoes. It is amazing how far a player with only a mediocre grasp of the game's finer points can progress in chess if his tactical play is sharp enough. Among the world's strongest players, those with the greatest strategical talents will ultimately come out on top; this is only because they are all, without exception, superb tacticians. Many a game between grandmasters is decided when one overlooks a relatively simple combination and the other seizes the chance to polish him off.

It is, of course, imperative to form a sound plan in accordance with the requirements of your position and to carry it through consistantly, but it is perhaps even more important to vary your play in accordance with the constantly varying tactical situation. To put the idea in simpler terms: suppose you are playing a particular game to gain an advantage in space on the Queenside and have made several moves in keeping with this plan. You are about to make yet another when you discern that your opponent has left his Queen *en prise* to one of your Pawns. Now the move PxQ makes no contribution whatsoever toward your immediate strategical objective, but it wins the game, and you should play it immediately—if not sooner. The whole business may appear too obvious to mention, but the idea does have its subtler applications. There are too many instances in chess history where a top master overlooked the chance to win his opponent's Queen because he was too deeply engrossed in profound strategical reflections to notice the present his opponent, likewise engrossed, had made him. There is an old anti-intellectual joke, first related by Plato (!) about the still-earlier Greek philosopher Thales who fell into a ditch while walking through a field because he was too busy staring up at the heavens to notice what was under his feet. Of course just as scholars are most often not only more scholarly but also more alert than other people, so real chess masters will usually see not only the difficult things in their games but the obvious things as well—though not always.

The distinction that we are making here between tactics (calculation of specific combinations) and strategy (the formation of an overall plan) came rather late into chess parlance even though it is in origin a war game, and the distinction between tactics and strategy in war ought to have suggested it from the first. The reason that it did not is to be found in the historical evolution of chess from the time of the last major rule changes, introduced in Italy toward the end of the fifteenth century. The most important of these changes vastly increased the power of the Queen from one of the weakest pieces to far and away the strongest. The new powers of the Queen immediately transformed the game from one of slow maneuvering to one of bold and daring thrust and counterthrust.

Because they had originated the new rules—which took more than a hundred years to gain acceptance throughout the rest of Europe—the Italians quickly took the lead in the development of a new style of play that afforded them a superiority to the rest of the world's players lasting until the eighteenth century. That style consisted wholly in attack against the enemy King. From the outset each player would mass his forces in the general direction of the hostile monarch, and the player who mated first was the winner. Giacchino Greco, the best known player of the seventeenth century, has come down to us primarily as the author of a series of flashy, but mostly unsound, mating combinations which have been preserved in a contemporary manuscript. Whether he actually played them over the board, or whether they are merely analysis, remains a mystery.

In the eighteenth century the balance of chess power shifted to France, where François André Danican Philidor temporarily revolutionized the game by teaching that it was the Pawn formation that determined the character of any given position, and that proper play with the Pawns was the key to success. "The pawn," as he put it with typical Gallic extravagance, "is the soul of chess." Philidor not only preached the primacy of Pawn play, but practiced what he preached, and his games are characterized by a ponderous maneuvering similar to that necessary before the Italian rules changes created the modern game. Nevertheless, his ideas had obvious merit, and throughout a long lifetime, in which he combined a highly productive career as a composer of music with his activities as a chess player, he proved himself again and again the best player of his time.

After he died, however, although France remained chessically the most powerful country in the world, the emphasis reverted once again to attack with the pieces in the manner of the Italian school. Players were out for excitement, and to them excitement meant attack, no matter how unjustified by the position and no matter what the cost in material. The French notables of the early nineteenth century, particularly Deschapelles and his pupil Labordonais, as well as other lesser players in France and elsewhere, believed and propagated the notion that any approach to the game other than a dashing straightforward attack against the opponent's King was not only useless but also unsportsmanlike.

It remained possible, for a long while, for the best players to continue in this vein chiefly because so few people possessed even elementary tactical ability—despite all the attention that had been lavished on that aspect of the game down through the centuries. Most club players today know more about tactics than the victims of the slashing attacks with which the top stars of the early nineteenth century made their reputations. Even among the top players themselves, defensive techniques were extremely crude and hence largely unavailing. As the game grew in popularity, however, the number of players who could conduct both a competent attack and a rudimentary defense rose steadily. More important, some players found no fun in being mated, however brilliantly, and focused their attentions, to an ever-increasing extent, on defensive techniques.

Thus it was that by the time of the first modern tournament, held in London in 1851, an event that inaugurated international competition as we know it, players were beginning to adopt a far more sophisticated approach to the game. Of those who took part, however, only the tournament winner, a German mathematics instructor named Adolf Anderssen, could be called even a tolerable strategist by today's standards. The name Anderssen has come down to us as almost synonymous with brilliancy, and indeed he is the author of some of the most intricate and ingenious attacking games of all time. But he had far more going for him than that: he could be cautious when necessary, he could play endgames, and, most interesting of all, he could defend much better than any of his contemporaries. Anderssen, in short, was the first player in chess history who could consistently adjust his plan to the needs of the position at hand, although even he lapsed on occasion into the old, bad attack-at-any-cost style. This willingness to adjust one's ideas to the requirements of the given situation, rather than attempting to impose one's will on it, is the beginning of all sound chess strategy.

Anderssen's conquerer, Paul Morphy, who came to Europe in 1857 from his native New Orleans and swept all before him, brought with him from the New World a further advance in chess technique. Morphy, like Anderssen, inherited from his predecessors a lust for attack and, again like Anderssen, was able to subordinate it when the situation demanded. He was, moreover, the first to thoroughly understand what we may call the strategical basis for tactical play. He was for a time the only player in the world who knew what every good player today takes for granted: that brilliant combinations arise logically out of previous play; and that the way to prepare for them was to achieve a rapid and harmonious development of one's pieces. This Morphy strove to accomplish from the outset. He introduced many new moves in well-known openings that had as their objective to place the pieces as effectively as possible in the shortest possible time. Morphy's whole career lasted for only a decade, and his most productive period for only about two years, but his notions about the game were so fruitful, and his results so impressive, that he effected a thoroughgoing transformation in chess technique. The game as we know it would be unthinkable without him.

The same may be said, and far more easily documented, of Wilhelm Steinitz, the first man in chess history ever to claim the world championship. Unlike Morphy, he put his ideas about the game down on paper and taught by exposition as well as by example. Steinitz was born May 17, 1836 (or, according to Dr. Neustadtl, May 14, 1835) in Prague, at that time part of the

Austro-Hungarian empire, of a very poor family, and spent several years of his young manhood living from hand to mouth as a chess professional. He began by playing for small stakes in the coffeehouses of Vienna, then a major chess center, but the best way to make a living at chess in those days was to find a patron. Since patrons of the nineteenth century were attracted largely by daring, sacrificial play, Steinitz cultivated a wild devil-may-care style, characterized by gambit openings and superficially complicated, predominantly tactical middle-games. He soon discovered what Morphy had realized almost instinctively: that to succeed at the highest level it is necessary to temper one's flights of fancy to the requirements of sober positional play; that against strong opposition one must lay the groundwork for one's attacks by slow and careful preparation.

There is an old adage, amusing to reflect on if not quite hagiographically sound, that every saint was a sinner in his youth, and Steinitz, after he became world champion, looked back on the sinful tactics (or was it the tactical sins) of his formative years with perhaps more antipathy than was warranted. Not only did he become an inveterate foe of gambit (sacrificial openings), doing much by his analytical powers and example to banish many of. the more unsound of them from serious play, but toward the end of his career came completely to subordinate tactical considerations in favor of strategical ones. This required not less attention to tactics, but more the willingness to allow his opponents more and more scope for their own operations in exchange for certain strategical objectives.

In simple terms this meant that he would allow his adversary a fierce attack in exchange for material. In chess one makes a sacrifice by exchanging material for time in the hope that that time can be utilized to advantage, to eventually win back the material with interest or to win outright by a direct assault against the enemy King. Steinitz was glad to accept his opponents' sacrifices, and then strive to ward off the ensuing attack, simplify, and come down to the endgame with a winning material advantage. In practice, Steinitz would go to enormous lengths to provoke his opponents into premature aggression, often taking on painfully constricted positions and allowing the most dangerous-looking attacks against his King. More often than not he would completely ignore various practical problems. The constant vigilance required to defend successfully, especially under the pressure of the time limit, occasionally took its toll, and sometimes he would forge a strategical masterpiece only to lose it all at the last moment by some tactical blunder in time pressure.

Steinitz, however, was nothing if not stubborn, and a misfortune in one game would never dissuade him from a path he thought theoretically correct. It remained for Emanuel Lasker (1868–1941), Steinitz' successor to the world championship, to combine strategy with tactics in a way that took into account not only theoretical problems but practical problems as well. Lasker was always willing to take some, often considerable, risks, but always after he had weighed the risk carefully against the chance and extent of possible gain. Lasker's schema, which relies heavily on the kind of tactical opportunism described earlier, has not yet been improved on except in matters of detail. Its most successful modern-day exponent is the present world champion Bobby Fischer.

The foregoing capsule history of tactical style provides something of a backdrop against which to see the intention of Fred Reinfeld's admirable book *The Secret of Tactical Chess* a bit more clearly. Perhaps never again in his amazingly prolific career did Reinfeld write a book so limited in scope, and yet so useful. Its subject is tactics, or perhaps more accurately the kind of tactical opportunism that is so salient a characteristic of modern master chess. The book is not intended as a complete chess course, although it does contain lucid introductory chapters on various aspects of the game intended primarily for the beginner, but rather it is designed to make the student aware of various tactical situations that occur again and again and of the ways in which he can turn such situations to his own advantage. It attempts to teach *alertness*, that quality without which all other chess virtues are well-nigh useless.

In chess, as in life, ontogeny reduplicates phylogeny. The beginner, as soon as he gets over his initial bewilderment at the complexity of the action taking place on the chessboard, goes through a period of preoccupation with tactics, and only gradually comes round to an appreciation of the finer points of strategy. The tactical foundation must be well laid, however, and, in the assistance it provides toward the laying of that foundation, this book, by a great chess teacher, has never been bettered.

THE SECRET OF TACTICAL CHESS

1. *Fundamentals*

Chess is often called "the royal game," partly because it was once played by kings, partly because it is the king of games. Over the centuries, no other game has equaled the perennial appeal of chess.

The chief reason for this is, I think, that it is the most intensely competitive of all games. It is at once complex and delicate, endlessly rich in resources for both players. Two well-matched players can fight on for hours, yet it is possible to force checkmate (against incredibly weak play) in only two moves!

Chess is a deeply creative hobby, worlds apart from the torpid watching of flickering images on a little screen. Chess gives us all the fun of a good fight, with none of the catastrophic penalties that follow defeat in real life. Because chess is so absorbing, it takes one's mind off troubles and difficulties; it refreshes and relaxes us, so that we can return to the workaday world with renewed vigor and ability.

Psychoanalysis tells us that chess is a good way of getting rid of our aggressive instincts, of letting off steam. I think this is borne out in actual experience.

Chess has been subjected to several myths which need puncturing. One of the most prevalent is that some people become chess addicts, neglecting wife, children, job. I have played chess and known chessplayers for thirty-five years, and have not yet come across an instance of this kind. I *have* known people who passionately loved chess who were famous authors, eminent scientists, distinguished professionals in many fields, and the like. So I would say that the myth of the chess addict belongs to the same category of American folklore as does the myth of the absentminded professor.

Some people avoid chess because they think it is a very difficult game, or because it is difficult to play well, or because it requires intelligence far beyond the ordinary. These are misconceptions.

There is no such thing as playing chess well by some absolute standard. Each chessplayer can consider himself a good or bad player merely in relation to the playing strength of his opponents. Chess of course requires intelligence; so do a great many other accomplishments which do not terrify us. For example, the person who can drive a car, play a musical instrument, or balance a check book need not be terrified by some purely imaginary standard of excellence he has set up for chessplaying.

My experience has been, by the way, that in chess great determination is more important than a high I.Q. Highly intelligent but careless or feckless people will lose out in the long run to the player with greater fighting spirit and determination. I think one of the great *practical* lessons to be learned from chess is that our capacity for putting up with adversity is much greater than we think it is.

To such questions as, "Can everyone play chess? Safely?" I can only answer, "Yes, why not?" I have known a great many people who derive enormous pleasure and sometimes profit from chess. I have never known anyone who was harmed by it.

Though chess is popularly supposed to be thousands of years old, the best evidence indicates that it started in India about 600 A.D. Rapidly spreading throughout Asia, it was cultivated by the Arabs, who introduced it in all their conquered territories. In time chess reached Spain, Italy, France, and other European countries.

The golden age of chess really started late in the eighteenth century. Subsequently, with the introduction of matches and tournaments, the popularity of the game increased mightily. One result has been that the literature devoted to chess is more extensive than the writings on all other games combined.

Let us turn now to chess itself, to review its basic rules rapidly.

One player has the White (light-colored) pieces; his opponent has the Black (dark-colored) pieces.

There are sixteen chessmen on a side. They are set up in the beginning in this fashion:

BLACK

DIAGRAM 1

WHITE

White always moves first, and the players take turns in making moves. To set up the board correctly, bear in mind that the right-hand corner square nearest the White player must be a white square.

Each player has two Rooks, which look like towers or castles. (They are sometimes called "castles," but if you want to sound sophisticated, call them "Rooks.") These are placed in the corner squares nearest each player.

Next to the Rooks, on the same horizontal row, we have the Knights. Each player has two Knights, and they are easy to recognize – they are horses.

Next to the Knights, and still on the same horizontal row, come the Bishops. They are also fairly easy to recognize, as they have tops (generally with a slit in them) which remind us of a bishop's miter.

Now we have to fill in the two center squares on this first horizontal row. First take the Queen – the second tallest piece, with a crown like a coronet. If you have the White Queen, place her on the empty white square on the horizontal row we have been filling.

As for the Black Queen, she will occupy the empty black square directly opposite all the way across the board. (If you have trouble visualizing this, look at the position of the Queens in Diagram 1.)

For the first row, the rest is easy enough. If you've followed directions so far, you're left with the two Kings – the tallest pieces of all, with crowns that are generally topped with a little cross. Place the White King next to the White Queen, and place the Black King next to the Black Queen.

Now you should have the first horizontal row on either side fully occupied. Check the situation with Diagram 1 before we go any further.

What remains? Each side still has eight Pawns – these are small, with rounded tops. The Pawns are set out on the eight squares of the second row, directly in front of the pieces. Again, check this with Diagram 1.

(Before we go on, a word of advice. Nowadays one often sees handsome – and expensive – sets designed in "modernistic" format. Such chessmen are attractive but highly impractical, especially for a player who is not too familiar with the chess pieces and their powers. In buying a set, you do well to stick to the old, familiar, Stauntonian pattern.)

Before we see how the chessmen move and capture, let's consider this problem: how do we record moves? how do we reproduce a given position?

The second question is easy to answer: we use diagrams, like the one you have just seen of the opening position, to reproduce any given situation on the board. This is your frame of reference where we are studying specific positions.

To record moves, we have to know what piece is moving and where it is moving to. Thus each chessman must have a name, and each square on the board must have a name.

So we turn to the board, noting that it has eight rows of eight squares, whether you look at it horizontally or vertically. All the squares are used – the white (light-colored) squares as well as the black (dark-colored) squares.

The horizontal rows on the board are known as "ranks." The vertical rows are known as "files." These two types of rows give us the coordinates we need for naming the squares.

Thus, White's King stands on his first rank. He also stands on a file which is called the King file, because both Kings are placed on it at the beginning of the game. Therefore, White's name for the square his King stands on is "King 1."

The White Bishop next to White's King is the "King Bishop" and White's name for the square his King Bishop stands on is "King Bishop 1." Then we have White's King Knight on "King Knight 1," and White's King Rook at King Rook 1.

As for White's Queen, she stands on White's "Queen 1" square, flanked by his Queen Bishop at his "Queen Bishop 1" square, his Queen Knight on his "Queen Knight 1" square, and his Queen Rook at his "Queen Rook 1" square.

Starting at White's extreme right, these squares are conveniently abbreviated in this way:

KR1; KN1 (or KKt1); KB1; K1; Q1; QB1; QN1 (or QKt1); QR1.

Each Pawn is named for the piece in front of which it stands. Or you might say each Pawn is named for the file on which it stands. Referring to Diagram 1, you will also note that all the White Pawns are placed on White's *second* rank.

Starting from White's extreme right, we have his King Rook Pawn (KRP); King Knight Pawn (KNP or KKtP); King Bishop Pawn (KBP); King Pawn (KP); Queen Pawn (QP); Queen Bishop Pawn (QBP); Queen Knight Pawn (QNP or QKtP); Queen Rook Pawn (QRP).

The squares on which these Pawns stand are respectively named from White's side of the board: KR2; KN2 (or KKt2); KB2; K2; Q2; QB2; QN2 (or QKt2); QR2.

(As you have noted, "N" is easier to write and use for "Knight" than is "Kt," and there is less chance of confusing it with K. Consequently "N" is becoming the standard abbreviation.)

So far all this has been very easy. But some people encounter a problem when we come to the Black side of the Board. So remember this: *When we record a White move, we count the ranks from White's side of the board. But when we record a Black move, we count the ranks from Black's side of the board.*

Diagram 2 shows how each square on the board has two names — a *White* name and a *Black* name.

BLACK

QR1 QR8	QN1 QN8	QB1 QB8	Q1 Q8	K1 K8	KB1 KB8	KN1 KN8	KR1 KR8
QR2 QR7	QN2 QN7	QB2 QB7	Q2 Q7	K2 K7	KB2 KB7	KN2 KN7	KR2 KR7
QR3 QR6	QN3 QN6	QB3 QB6	Q3 Q6	K3 K6	KB3 KB6	KN3 KN6	KR3 KR6
QR4 QR5	QN4 QN5	QB4 QB5	Q4 Q5	K4 K5	KB4 KB5	KN4 KN5	KR4 KR5
QR5 QR4	QN5 QN4	QB5 QB4	Q5 Q4	K5 K4	KB5 KB4	KN5 KN4	KR5 KR4
QR6 QR3	QN6 QN3	QB6 QB3	Q6 Q3	K6 K3	KB6 KB3	KN6 KN3	KR6 KR3
QR7 QR2	QN7 QN2	QB7 QB2	Q7 Q2	K7 K2	KB7 KB2	KN7 KN2	KR7 KR2
QR8 QR1	QN8 QN1	QB8 QB1	Q8 Q1	K8 K1	KB8 KB1	KN8 KN1	KR8 KR1

WHITE

DIAGRAM 2

Studying Diagram 2, you will note that in the opening position, all the Black pieces are situated on squares in the Black camp which are named just like the corresponding squares in the White camp.

All this makes good sense. If you play the piano, you will recall that the same note may have a different name depending on the key signature. Thus, C sharp and D flat are one and the same note. Similarly, White's K4 and Black's K5 are one and the same square.

Now here is an important precaution. When we record moves, or when we set them out in a book, we have to be very careful to show the reader whether it is a White move or a Black move.

We do this by setting the moves in two vertical columns. The moves in the left column are White's moves. The moves in the right column are Black's moves. Each Black move is kept on the same horizontal level as the preceding White move. Take this sequence:

WHITE	BLACK
1 **P–K4**	**P–K4**
2 **N–KB3**	**N–QB3**
3 **B–B4**	**B–B4**

What does this mean? First White played P–K4, and Black replied *1* .... P–K4. (Note that when we give moves in the body of the text, we always place four periods before a Black move to distinguish it from a White move.)

To return to the game: White's second move was 2 N–KB3, to which Black replied *2* .... N–QB3. White's third move was *3* B–B4, to which Black's reply was *3* .... B–B4. The subsequent moves of the game will continue to be noted down in the same way.

Before we leave the chess notation, here are a few more symbols and abbreviations which you will find useful.

x	(captures)
–	(moves to)

!	(a good move)
!!	(a very good move)
?	(a bad move)
??	(a very bad move)
?! or !?	(a move which has good and bad features)
ch	(check)
dis ch	(discovered check)
dbl ch	(double check)
O–O	(castles on the King-side)
o–o–o	(castles on the Queen-side)
e.p.	(captures en passant, or in passing)
/	(used to avoid ambiguity, as R/K2–K6; also used to indicate Pawn promotion, as P–Q8/Q)

Now for the powers of the pieces.

The King moves one square in any direction. He can capture any hostile force in his moving range. (Thus, if White's King is at King Knight 2, he can move to King Knight 1, King Rook 1, King Rook 2, King Rook 3, King Knight 3, King Bishop 3, King Bishop 2, King Bishop 1. He can also capture any hostile forces on those squares.) This is shown in Diagram 3.

BLACK

DIAGRAM 3

WHITE

In all references to capturing, remember that in chess, capturing pieces *do not* leap over the captured piece. Instead, the capturing piece *displaces* the captured piece.

In the discussion on page 18, you will see that there are times when the King cannot make certain moves or captures that are inside his moving range.

The Queen, like the King, moves in all directions, one *or* more squares at a time, whichever she wants. The only obstacles are her own pieces or the opponent's pieces which may be on those lines. Thus, if the White Queen is at White's King 5 square, as in Diagram 4, she has a choice of 27 possible moves.

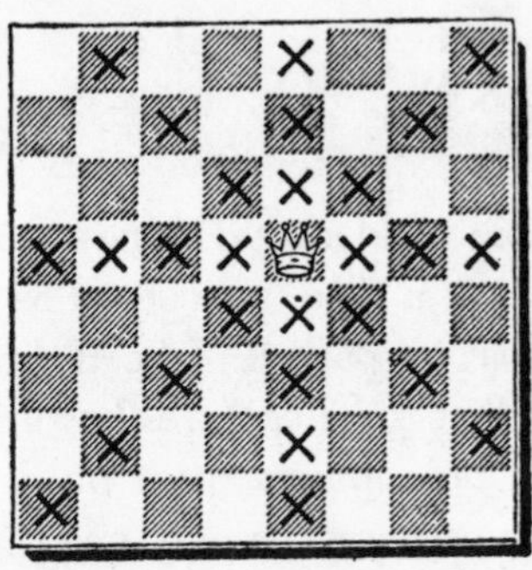

DIAGRAM 4

The Queen captures the same way that she moves; vertically, horizontally, or diagonally. (A "diagonal" is a row of squares of the same color which touch each other only at their corners. For example, reckoning from the White side, the squares Queen Rook 1, Queen Knight 2, Queen Bishop 3, Queen 4, King 5, King Bishop 6, King Knight 7, and King Rook 8 form a diagonal. Note this diagonal on Diagram 4.)

Of course, when we say that the Queen can move in any direction, she can move in only *one* direction on any *one* move. Similarly, though she may be in position to capture several pieces, she can take only *one* at any given turn. This applies to all the chessmen as well.

The Rook has *two* of the Queen's powers.

The Rook can move horizontally or vertically, one *or* more squares at a time. It can make any capture – by displacement, of course — that is in its moving range. The Rook's moving powers are shown in Diagram 5.

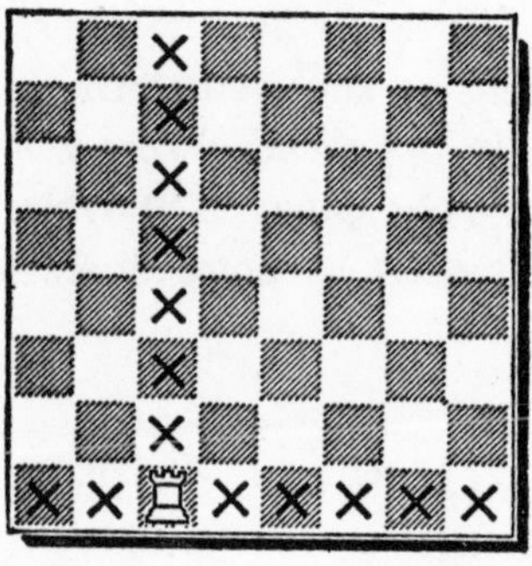

DIAGRAM 5

The Bishop's move takes some pondering. He moves only on diagonals, one *or* more squares at a time, whichever he wants. (See the definition of a diagonal on page 9.) The Bishop captures the same way he moves: that is, he captures hostile forces within his moving range, and he captures them by displacement. Of course, he moves (or captures) in only one direction at a time. In Diagram 6 we see the Bishop's diagonal possibilities.

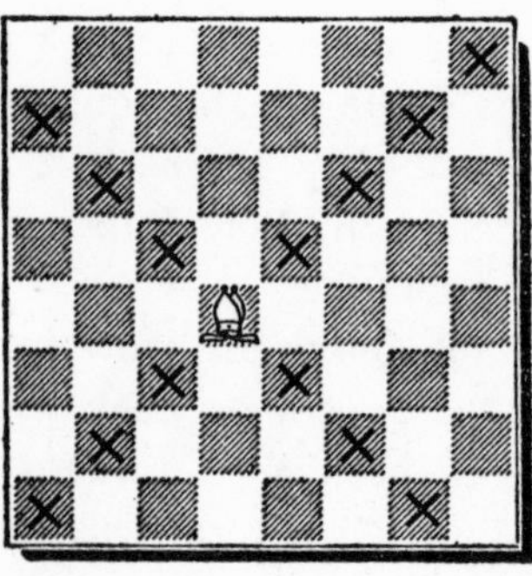

DIAGRAM 6

Now here is something about the Bishop's move that is worth noticing. The diagonals have this peculiarity, that all the squares on a diagonal are of one color. Some diagonals are white-square diagonals; the others are black-square diagonals.

One Bishop always travels on white-square diagonals; the other always travels on black-square diagonals. Consequently a Bishop can never capture hostile forces placed on the color which he does not command.

The Knight, in a sense, is a law unto himself. His move differs in certain significant respects from the moves of all the other chessmen, and you must therefore study it with special care.

Study Diagram 7, which shows a White Knight at White's King 5 square. Eight possible Knight moves are indicated. What is the principle on which they are based? Obviously, the moves are not horizontal, or vertical, or diagonal. What remains? This: *the Knight's move is a composite of movement in two combined directions.*

BLACK

DIAGRAM 7

WHITE

The Knight's move, we see on reflection, is "L"-shaped.

He moves one square in a horizontal direction, and then two more squares in a vertical direction.

Or, he moves one square in a vertical direction, and then two more squares in a horizontal direction.

Both concepts are valid, and both are needed to make possible the eight moves shown in Diagram 7.

One important way the Bishop and Knight differ is this: whereas the Bishop always travels on squares of the same color, the Knight *always* changes the color of the square he occupies. If he moves from a white square, he will land on a black square. If he moves from a black square, he will land on a white square.

The Knight can capture *only* on the terminal square of his move. He *cannot* capture hostile forces located on the intermediate squares of his move. He *can* leap over such pieces, but without capturing them. Likewise, he can leap over his own pieces, if they are on the intermediate squares of his move.

BLACK

DIAGRAM 8

WHITE

In Diagram 8, the White Knight can capture any of the Black Pawns. The Knight can leap over the White Pawn and the White Rook. The Knight can also leap over the Black Rook, but does not – cannot – capture it in so doing.

Since the Knight, unlike the Bishop, changes the color of his square every time he moves, he can sooner or later attack or occupy every square on the chessboard. In actual practice this does not happen, but it is possible.

The Pawn also has some interesting quirks. Unlike all the other chessmen, the Pawn can move only vertically forward. It can never retreat or move sideways. (Applying this to the reading of chess diagrams, we note the legend "WHITE" at the bottom of the diagram, which means that White Pawns always move up the page. The legend "BLACK" at the top of the diagram means that the Black Pawns always move downward.

Note the situation of the White and Black Pawns in Diagram 1.)

In Diagram 1, you observe that all the White Pawns are originally placed on White's second rank, while all the Black Pawns are originally placed on Black's second rank.

As long as a Pawn is on its original square on the second rank, it has the option of advancing *one* or *two* squares. Once any Pawn has moved, it can advance only one square. In Diagram 9 we see some possible Pawn moves.

DIAGRAM 9

Suppose it is White's move. He can advance his King Rook Pawn one square or two squares, as he pleases. What about White's King Pawn? It is blocked by Black's King Pawn, and cannot advance at all.

Finally, there is White's Queen Knight Pawn, which can advance *one* square to White's Queen Knight 5. (It is no longer on its original square, consequently it no longer has the option of advancing one square or two.)

As for Black, he can advance his King Knight Pawn or Queen Bishop Pawn or Queen Rook Pawn *one* square, if it is his move.

Note the far-advanced White Pawn at King Bishop 7. If it is White's move, he can advance this Pawn one square. But this involves a special case, which we shall deal with a little later.

The Pawn has this interesting peculiarity: it does *not* capture the same way it moves.

The Pawn *moves* straight ahead, as we have seen. But it captures one square forward *to the right or left*. In other words, the Pawn captures diagonally.

Specifically, in the situation in Diagram 9, if it is White's turn to move, he can capture Black's Queen Bishop Pawn or Queen Rook Pawn with the White Queen Knight Pawn.

If it is Black's turn to move, he can capture White's Queen Knight Pawn with his Queen Rook Pawn or with his Queen Bishop Pawn. But note that neither King Pawn can capture the other; the Pawns do not capture in that fashion.

The Pawn not only captures Pawns in the manner indicated; it also captures Bishop, Knight, Rook, and Queen in the same way.

Now let us return to Diagram 9 and consider the status of the White Pawn on King Bishop 7. Any Pawn so placed – that is, on its seventh rank – becomes a Queen when it advances to the eighth and last rank.

What happens is this: you advance the Pawn, remove it, and replace it with a Queen. Theoretically, each of your Pawns can become a Queen in this way. In actual play, the promotion of more than one Pawn in a game is highly unlikely.

We speak of "queening a Pawn" but this is not strictly accurate. Actually, you can promote the Pawn to a Queen, Rook, Knight, or Bishop – whichever you please. The Queen is the piece chosen in the vast majority of cases because it is by far the most powerful (see page 20).

Now for one more facet of Pawn play: capturing in passing, or *en passant*. This is a power or option possessed only by the Pawn; and it applies only to cases where a *Pawn* can capture a *Pawn*.

Turn back once more to Diagram 9. Suppose White advances his King Rook Pawn *one square*. In that case, Black can capture this Pawn with his King Knight Pawn.

But suppose that White advances his King Rook Pawn *two squares*. Then Black has the right – not the duty – to capture White's King Rook Pawn "in passing" – *as if* the King Rook

Pawn had advanced *only one square.* True to this concept, Black's King Knight Pawn after this capture ends up on Black's King Rook 6.

Now to recapitulate:

The Pawn which is to be captured must be on its second rank. The hostile Pawn that is to recapture must be on its fifth rank, and on a file *adjacent* to the file of the Pawn that will advance to the *en passant* position.

Now, when the first Pawn advances two squares, the hostile Pawn can capture it as if it had advanced one square. The capture is optional, but if it is to be executed at all, it must be done *in reply* to the advance of the first Pawn. If the option is turned down, it cannot be resumed later on.

In all cases, we have seen that you can move only one piece at a time. There is just one exception, and that is the combination move known as castling. This is done with the King and a Rook. So we have King-side castling or Queen-side castling. Diagrams 10 and 11 show how this is accomplished.

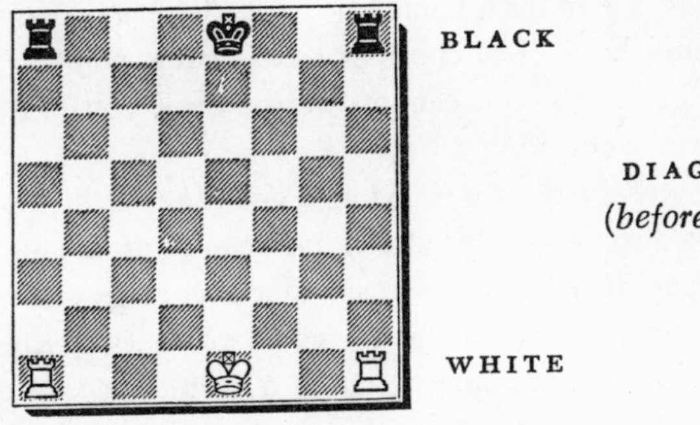

DIAGRAM **10**
(before castling)

To castle with the King Rook, White moves his King two squares in the direction of his King Rook. Then he places his Rook to the immediate left of his King. (Castling with the Black

King is the same, except that you move the Black King to your left, and the Black King Rook to your right.)

To castle with the Queen Rook, White moves his King two squares to the left and places his Queen Rook to the immediate right of his King. (To castle with his Queen Rook, Black moves his King two squares to the right and places his Queen Rook to the immediate left of his King.)

Note once more that this twofold move is considered a single move. Diagram 11 shows the situation after castling on either wing.

DIAGRAM 11
(*after castling*)

There are a number of limitations on the castling privilege, and it would be well to consider them at this point.

In the first place, you cannot ever castle if you have previously moved your King.

Nor can you castle if your King is under attack by an enemy piece. However, when this attack has been parried, and if your King has not moved, you can castle at a later stage of the game.

You cannot castle if doing so would place your King on a square within the attacking range of a hostile piece. However, if that menace is removed and all the other conditions are satisfactory, you may then castle.

Likewise, you cannot castle if your King has to pass over squares within the attacking range of a hostile piece. Here too, when the attack is neutralized or removed, you can castle if you satisfy all the other requirements.

Finally, in order to castle you cannot leap over your own or enemy pieces. The squares your King and Rook pass over must be empty, as they are in Diagram 10. If they are occupied, you can castle later on if the intervening squares become empty and all other castling requirements are satisfied.

How do you win a game of chess? What are the basic requirements? Basically, you win a game of chess by *checkmating* the opposing King. This is done by attacking the hostile King so that he cannot escape. Checkmate is described in great detail in Chapter 3, so we need not dwell on it unduly at this point. Right now, the vital aspect for you to concentrate on is that the King is *uniquely valuable*. If you lose your Queen, the strongest of all the pieces, you can still play on. But if your King is trapped without any way of escape, the game ends right then and there.

This does not mean that every game *necessarily* ends with checkmate. For example, if a player loses a great deal of material and knows that checkmate is inevitable, he may concede defeat by "resigning." In fact, many games end this way.

An attack on the King is known as a "check." It is conventional, though not required, to announce "check." (By an "attack on the King" we mean a hostile move that places the King within the capturing range of a hostile piece.) By way of example, note that in Diagram 16 White's Rook is checking the Black King.

When a King is checked, something must be done about it. (If nothing *can* be done, then the King is checkmated, and the game is over.)

How can a King get out of check? There are three ways. One way is to capture the checking piece. Another way is to interpose one of your pieces along the line of attack. The third way is to move your King off the line of attack. In each of these three ways you get your King out of check. (Note, by the way, that it is illegal to *voluntarily* place your King in check.)

Most games end in checkmate or else in resignation by the weaker side. Some games, however, end in a "draw." This means that neither side wins.

Some games are drawn by agreement. If neither player sees a chance to win, a draw can be agreed on. In fact, the players can agree to a draw if they feel like it, even though one of them may have the objective assets that make a win possible.

Secondly, a game may be drawn by perpetual check. This is a position where a player can check at will repeatedly, while his opponent is unable to put an end to the series of checks. Usually the player who is giving the perpetual check insists on taking the draw because he has some overriding disadvantage, such as a deficiency in material. Obviously he is better off to take a draw than risk losing because he is behind in material.

Third, a game can be called a draw if one of the players can demonstrate that no piece has been captured and no Pawn moved in the last 50 moves. This rule is conceived as a penalty against the player who has a big plus in material but who lacks the skill to force checkmate. The rule is rarely invoked, since it presupposes a written record of the game; and few players are sufficiently well versed in chess notation to keep a written record.

Fourth, a draw may be claimed if a position has already occurred twice, and is about to recur a third time. This type of draw, like the previous one, is rare because it presupposes the existence of a written record. Without such a written record, one cannot prove one's claim if it is disputed by the other player.

Finally, games can be drawn by stalemate. This happens fairly often in the games of inexperienced players. It is of crucial importance to distinguish between *checkmate* and *stalemate,* a distinction which baffles many players.

Checkmate refers to a position in which the player whose turn it is to move, is in check and cannot get out of check.

Stalemate refers to a position in which the player whose turn it is to move is *not* in check; yet he finds himself in a situation where any move he makes will expose him to check. (For detailed discussion of such situations, see page 72.)

To give you some orientation on how to checkmate, we may say that this is *generally* achieved by gaining a preponderance of material – that is, by winning more of your opponent's pieces than you lose in return. When you have more power for attack than your opponent has for defense, the chances are all in your favor that you can *force* checkmate no matter what your opponent does.

This also works in another way: when you are ahead in material, you can exchange piece for piece with a view to reaching one of the basic checkmating positions that are described in detail in Chapter 3.

In order to know how to win material, or to know when you are ahead in material, or behind in material, or even in material, you need to know the values of the pieces, and *their value in relation to each other*. For example, is it advisable to capture a Bishop if you have to give up a Rook for it? Should you give up your Queen if you can win two Rooks and a Knight in return?

Any player who does not have a good, immediate answer to these questions is seriously handicapped. Long experience has shown that a highly reliable table of arbitrary values may be assigned to the different pieces:

Queen	**9 points**
Rook	**5 points**
Bishop	**3 points**
Knight	**3 points**
Pawn	**1 point**

(Note that we exclude the King as his preservation is absolutely essential.)

This table gives us a lot of valuable information which clears away many of the confusing aspects of chess. By applying this table, we can often decide at once whether a given capture is advisable or not.

For example, if Bishop and Knight are of equal value, we can readily exchange one for the other.

On the other hand, the Queen is so valuable that we would not dream of exchanging her for a mere Rook or Bishop or Knight. Note this: if you win your opponent's Queen in return for a Rook, say, you have gained an enormous plus in material and should win easily with your superior force.

If you have a Rook in return for a minor piece (Bishops and Knights are known as "minor" pieces) you are ahead in material. Such an advantage is known as being "the Exchange ahead." Even if you have a Rook (5 points) against a minor piece and Pawn (4 points), you are still ahead in material. If you have a Rook (5 points) against a minor piece and two Pawns (5 points), material is even, and the decision will depend on the special aspects of any given position.

Note that a Queen (9 points) has the upper hand against a Rook and minor piece (a total of 8 points). Two Rooks (10 points) are stronger than a Queen (9 points).

All this is rather abstract, and it is often modified by the nature of the individual position. For example, a Pawn on the seventh rank, poised to move on to the queening square, is obviously much more powerful than a Pawn on its original square.

Despite these differences, the table is extraordinarily helpful, especially at the beginning of the game. Take the situation in Diagram 12, for example.

BLACK

DIAGRAM 12

WHITE *to play*

White can play NxP ?, but in that case Black replies . . . . PxN. The upshot is that White has given up a Knight (3 points) for a Pawn (1 point), obviously a very bad transaction. Our conclusion, therefore, is that in the position of Diagram 12 White should avoid NxP ?

(Note an interesting point here. Black's Queen Pawn does a very fine defensive job. Pawns make wonderful defenders because they are the least valuable of all the chessmen. To use the formidable Queen for the same purpose would be woefully uneconomical.)

In Diagram 13 we have an instructive situation. White has won the Exchange: he has a Rook for a Knight. What does this advantage mean in concrete terms?

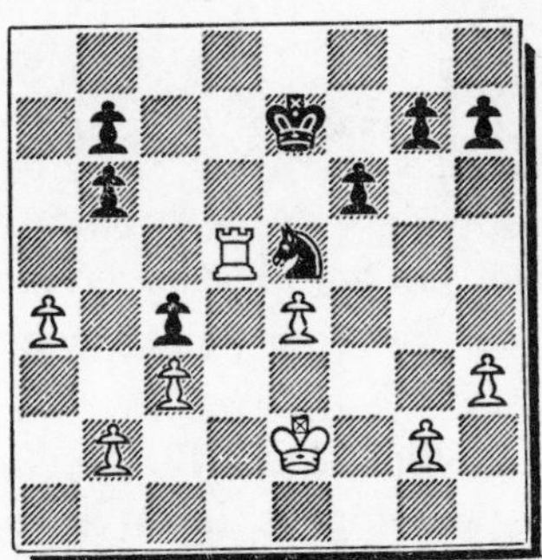

BLACK

DIAGRAM 13

WHITE *to play*

The Rook is stronger than the Knight *because the Rook has greater mobility than the Knight.* The Rook can reach more squares and attack more efficiently than the Knight can defend. White proves the point by playing:

1 **R–N5** ....

Attacking the Black Pawn at Black's Queen Knight 3.

1 .... **N–Q2**

He defends the attacked Pawn. (Now, obviously, White would not dream of *2* RxP ?? because of *2* .... NxR.)

2 **R–N4 !** ....

This wins a Pawn, for if Black plays 2 .... N–K4 he relinquishes the protection of his Queen Knight Pawn.

Thus we see that the Rook can simultaneously attack the two Pawns, while the Knight can defend them only one at a time. This gives us some idea of what it means to be the Exchange ahead.

In Diagram 14 we find a much more complicated situation.

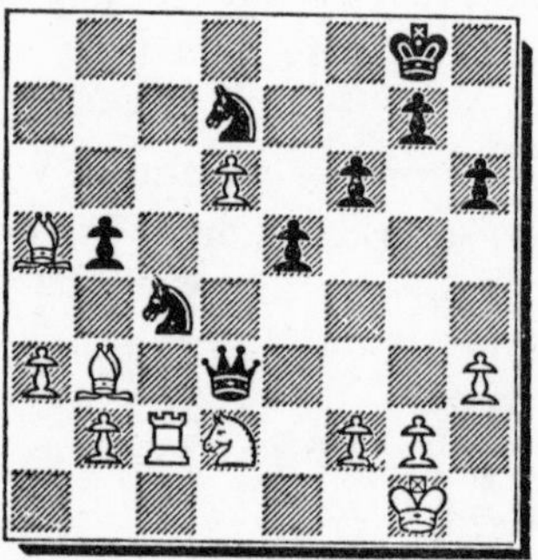

BLACK

DIAGRAM 14

WHITE *to play*

Consulting our table of values, we find that material is even: White has a Rook, Bishop, and Pawn (9 points) against the Black Queen (9 points).

An important feature of the position is that Black's Knight at Queen Bishop 5 is "pinned." It cannot move, for to do so would expose Black's King to attack by White's Bishop at Queen Knight 3.

White's move is astonishing:

1 RxN! ....

This leaves Black in an embarrassing dilemma. If he plays *1* .... PxR there follows 2 BxP ch with *double attack* on Black's King and Queen. Then, after 2 .... QxB; 3 NxQ, it turns out that White is a piece and Pawn to the good, with an easy win.

Suppose Black wants to answer *1* RxN! in some other way. For example, *1* .... Q–K7. Then White replies 2 R–K4 dis ch, giving check by moving his Rook and opening up the Bishop's line of fire along the diagonal, and at the same time attacking Black's Queen. *Black must get his King out of check,* so that White wins the Queen by force.

Suppose Black answers *1* RxN! with *1* .... K–B1. Then White replies 2 R–B8 mate, as 2 .... K–K2 is impossible.

Or if *1* RxN!, K–R1; 2 R–B8 ch, K–R2; 3 B–B2 winning by *pinning* Black's unfortunate Queen, which finds itself on the same diagonal as the Black King.

In all these possibilities we see the great power of *1* RxN! It is a *forcing move* because it is a *capture* and because it *threatens a check and the win of Black's Queen.*

So, by following the table of values, we know that after *1* RxN!, PxR; 2 BxP ch, White comes out ahead in material. We also know that on other Black moves White wins by means of forcing, violent moves. This will form the main subject matter of the book, beginning with Chapter 4.

Remember that being ahead in material does not *automatically* ensure your victory. You may blunder away your material advantage. Or else one little oversight, or some trick or trap or finesse, may enable your opponent to force checkmate in some freak manner.

This sword of Damocles, this constant potential threat that hangs over your King, calls for unremitting vigilance. No matter what you do or what you plan, you must look for the crude, violent possibilities that may exist in any given position.

At every move you must ask yourself: "Can I force checkmate? Can I win material? Can I capture something? Can I threaten something?" Also: "Is he threatening to force checkmate? Is he threatening to win material from me?"

Most players, especially inexperienced ones, are always worrying about the abstract possibility of looking ahead. To form general plans is fairly easy; to foresee specific moves is difficult. Practically all games are decided by the here and now, by what is possible *directly* in any given position.

This, by the way, is the material of the present book. The quickest way to improve your playing strength enormously is to train yourself to appraise the *immediate* possibilities that exist in any given position. This book has been written to give you that invaluable training.

Much of the charm of chess arises from its complexity, which in turn is derived from the disparate values of the different chessmen. Hence it is of prime importance to be familiar with the relative values of the chessmen. This has been explained with practical examples, beginning on page 20.

At this point we can observe that because the chessmen have different powers, they each have a distinctive "personality."

The beginner, for example, is enchanted with the Queen's enormous powers arising from her ability to move in all directions. In fact, he places so much faith in her that if he is confronted with the grim alternative of losing the Queen or being checkmated, he will choose the latter alternative – obviously a foolish decision.

Again, the exchange of Queens – giving up one's Queen for the opponent's Queen – is avoided by many players on the ground that the disappearance of the Queen deprives the game of its fascination. Some players will drive this point so hard that they will lose material rather than exchange Queens.

This too is a foolish foible, for material should never be given up without adequate or more than adequate compensation. Having criticized such extreme views, we can heartily commend a reasonable predilection for the Queen, for this powerful piece is usually the spearhead of the most artistic and satisfyingly brilliant strokes that are possible in chess.

The Queen's long-range attacking power is well illustrated in Diagram 15.

BLACK

DIAGRAM 15

WHITE

White is giving check with his Queen. Black cannot capture the Queen (she is guarded by the White Bishop). The Black King cannot run away. Consequently Black is checkmated.

This diagram also indicates vividly that the Queen generally operates most effectively in combination with one or more colleagues. It is instructive to see here, for example, how well the faraway White Bishop cooperates powerfully in White's attack. On the other hand, if the Queen is out of touch with the other pieces, as in Diagram 104, the consequences may be disastrous.

As regards the development of the Queen, she should not be brought out too early unless you can see some immediate, sizable advantage (such as a huge gain of material). Otherwise, when developed prematurely, she can be hounded by enemy pieces of lesser value.

The Rook presents a problem which is rarely solved by the inexperienced player because he is not even aware of the problem. Look at Diagram 1 and you will see that the Rooks in the corners are completely hemmed in by their own forces. Now, these Rooks must have mobility – freedom of action.

The only way the Rooks can get this mobility is by being placed on *open lines.* Then they display their power against the enemy, because they are no longer blocked. An important step for getting at least the King Rook into active play is castling. This at least brings the King Rook out of the corner where it is in danger of being buried for a good part of the game. (See Diagram 149 for an example of the Rook's power on an open line after castling.)

And remember this: *open lines are created by* Pawn captures. So, as soon as a file becomes opened, think of placing one of your Rooks on it. In this way you will enormously increase the striking power of the Rook.

The power of the Rook can be impressive, as shown in Diagram 13 or 16.

BLACK *to play*

DIAGRAM **16**

WHITE

White is giving check with his Rook, and he is also attacking Black's Bishop. If Black is foolish enough to move his King in order to get out of check, White replies RxB, winning a piece with an easy victory in sight. This shows the power of a Rook on an open line.

But Black has a better move:

1 .... **R–Q2**

By interposing with his Rook, Black gets his King out of check and also protects his Bishop. (If White plays 2 RxB ?, Black replies 2 .... RxR and Black has won the Exchange and should win the game; see the table of relative values on this point. So Black's Rook move also sets off the value of this piece in a favorable light.)

2 **RxBP** ....

Best; White wins a Pawn, and, since he is attacking both Black Rook Pawns, he will win at least another Pawn and eventually the game. Here too we can appreciate the power of the Rook.

The Bishop is particularly strong in "open" positions where the Pawns have been cleared away and the Bishop has full sway. Better yet, a pair of cooperating Bishops, commanding squares of both colors and concentrated against the opposing King, can often bring about remarkably brilliant play, or else choke the opponent to death, as happens in Diagram 148.

On the other hand, you must not allow yourself to be dazzled by the long-range powers of the Bishop on the diagonals. Many a beginner has been caught in the kind of trap shown in Diagram 17.

BLACK

DIAGRAM 17

WHITE *to play*

White sees that he can capture Black's Rook Pawn. Why not? The Pawn is not *directly* protected. So he plays BxP?; but now Black replies . . . . P–N3 and the miserable Bishop is trapped! On his next move Black will inexorably continue . . . . K–N2, forcing the win of the Bishop.

Unlike the Rook, the Bishop plays a prominent role in the opening. Once you advance your King Pawn two squares, you have created a path for the development of your King Bishop. In this connection, note that many beginners commit the fault of self-blocking. For example, if, after P–K4 you play P–Q3? before bringing out your King Bishop, then you have blocked the diagonal of your King Bishop and cut down his mobility very considerably.

Now, if your opponent develops his King Bishop favorably and you have limited the action of *your* King Bishop, you are at a disadvantage which may persist throughout the game. So, avoid Pawn moves which have a self-limiting effect on your Bishops.

Many players like to develop the King Bishop to Queen Bishop 4, producing a pattern shown in Diagram 18. This is a good idea, as the Bishop then bears down on the enemy's weakest point, his King Bishop Pawn.

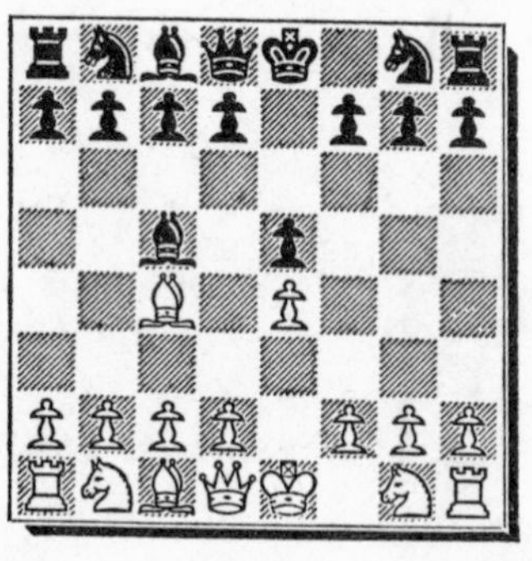

BLACK

DIAGRAM 18

WHITE

But this pattern becomes impossible after a premature P–Q3? Hence this self-blocking move is to be avoided.

Opinions of the Knight are quite discordant. It has its passionate champions and equally vehement detractors. The inexperienced player is apt to dislike the Knight because its unconventional "corkscrew" move is hard to fathom and hard to foresee.

Nevertheless, the Knight is capable of exquisite evolutions and its "forking" powers make it a frightful enemy that strikes with unexampled elegance and brute force. The play in Diagrams 80-85 will convince even the most case-hardened opponent.

In Diagram 19 we have a typical example of how an inexperienced player succumbs to a devastating Knight fork.

BLACK *to play*

DIAGRAM 19

WHITE

Black sees that he can win a Pawn by simply playing .... BxP.

What he overlooks is that his Bishop is playing a vital role in parrying the terrible forking possibility N–K6 ch with simultaneous attack on the Black King and Queen.

Black's proper course is to play some such move as .... Q–Q2, ending the forking possibility. In that case Black would truly be threatening .... BxP. Instead:

1	**BxP** ??
2 **N–K6** ch	....

This diabolical Knight fork wins Black's Queen.

But there is also a weaker side to the Knight's move which inexperienced players rarely recognize. This is the fact that the Knight moves in short hops. Consequently, if he is advanced too far, he may easily find himself out on a limb.

In Diagram 20, we have a situation in which the Knight overextends himself.

BLACK

DIAGRAM 20

WHITE *to play*

White's Knight is attacked by Black's Bishop. White should retreat – N–Q2, for example. Instead, he rushes after an apparently unprotected Pawn.

1 **NxP** ?? **K–N3** !

White's Knight is trapped – no escape! This illustrates the danger of letting the Knight wander too far afield.

In the opening, beginners are fond of playing the Knight to King Knight 5 (from King Bishop 3). This should only be done if the Knight is safe from attack at his new post. Besides, such an attack should be ventured only in combination with other pieces. If the attack is easily parried, it is not worth trying except against a very weak opponent.

Because the Pawns are the weakest of all the chess units, the inexperienced chessplayer is likely to despise them and apt to part with them with cavalier abandon. But this is all wrong, because the Pawns can be, and are, of great value. (One might compare them to the bacteria, which, despite their tiny size, are enormously harmful or useful to mankind.)

Much more often than we suspect, a single "lowly" Pawn decides the outcome of the game. You can see this for yourself in Diagrams 156-159.

And for a simple illustration of this situation, see what happens in Diagram 21.

BLACK

DIAGRAM 21

WHITE *to play*

White advances his Queen Bishop Pawn to the last row, and he can now promote it to a Queen, Rook, Knight, or Bishop. (This means that he removes the Pawn and replaces it with a new piece of his choice.) In this case, White promotes the Pawn to a Queen (or Rook), giving checkmate on the spot. The lowly Pawn has become a powerful piece.

Few beginners keep vividly before them this mighty transformation of the Pawn. But once this enormous increase in power is firmly ingrained in your chess thinking, you will have a vastly enhanced respect for the Pawn.

An age-old question is, "What is best, offensive or defensive play?" The answer is, "It all depends."

If you have brought out all your pieces, and they are well placed, by all means look for attacking possibilities. If your opponent has neglected to "develop" his pieces; if his position is cramped; if his King is exposed to attack; then again by all means look for attacking possibilities.

On the other hand, if your position is bad, you have problems of a different order. Thus, if you have lost valuable material – perhaps your Queen – in the opening, you have a hopeless fight on your hands. Unless your opponent is an extremely poor player, your wisest decision is to resign and start a new game.

But suppose your position is bad because you have neglected to develop (bring out) your pieces from their home squares. Then your predicament is not necessarily hopeless. If your opponent has similarly neglected to bring out *his* pieces, you are under no great pressure, and you can proceed to make good your previous omissions of development. Take Diagram 22 as an example.

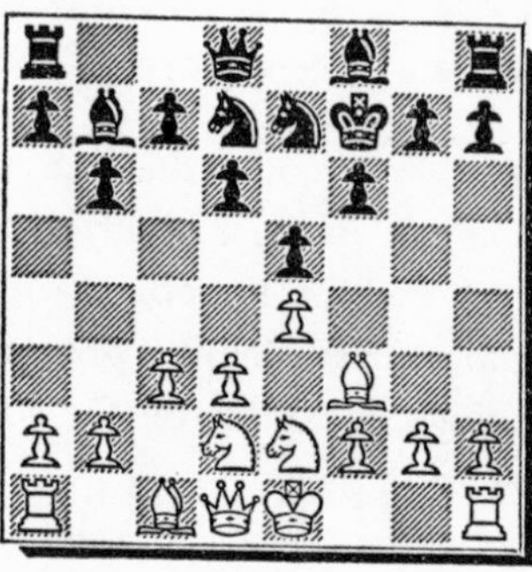

BLACK

DIAGRAM 22

WHITE *to play*

White has played poorly. His Bishop on King Bishop 3 has no scope. His King Knight should have gone to the more aggressive square King Bishop 3 instead of King 2. His other Knight blocks the development of his Queen Bishop. He has neglected to castle.

Yet – paradoxically! – his prospects are not bad! Because Black has also developed miserably. He has already moved his King, and will therefore not be able to castle. One Bishop is completely hemmed in, the other (at Queen Knight 2) has little scope. His Knights (like White's) have been developed colorlessly to King 2 and Queen 2 instead of more aggressively to King Bishop 3 and Queen Bishop 3 respectively.

So, to sum up, thanks to Black's poor play White is in no great danger. Many constructive vistas are still open to him. He can castle, and then play B–N4, improving the position of his King Bishop and preparing for P–KB4. This will cause Pawn exchanges and thus create an open file for his castled Rook. In addition he can post his Queen Knight more aggressively by moving it from Queen 2 to Queen Bishop 4. This will give the Knight pressure on the center, and will also open up the diagonal for the development of his Queen Bishop.

So we see in Diagram 22 that White can get off scot-free, despite his poor development, because Black's development has been even more inept.

But if you have developed badly in the opening and your opponent has developed quickly and aggressively, then you are in for trouble – serious trouble. See White's predicament in Diagram 23, for example.

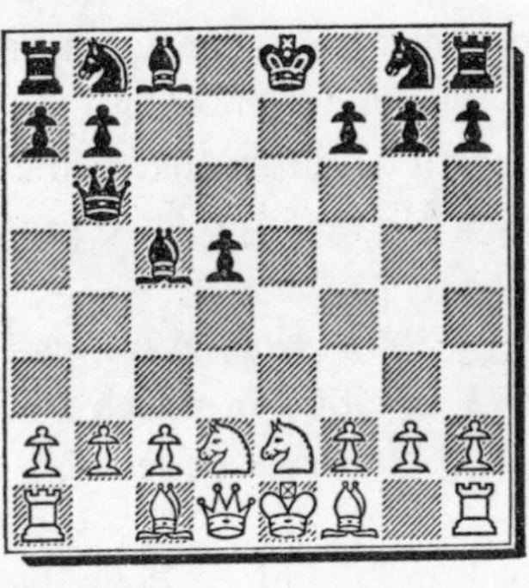

BLACK

DIAGRAM 23

WHITE *to play*

White has kept pace with Black in the matter of *quantitative* development – they each have two pieces out, and Black has advanced a Pawn. But qualitatively Black is far ahead, for White has played two puny self-blocking moves – play your Knights to the third rank and not the second! – while Black has played two aggressive moves that strike at the very heart of White's position.

Though only six moves have been made on each side, White's position is desperate beyond repair. Already Black threatens an immediate .... BxP mate, and thanks to White's self-blocking moves, he can ward off this disaster only by heavy material loss.

Thus, *1* N–KB3? or *1* N–QN3? will not serve because of *1* .... BxP ch; *2* K–Q2, Q–K6 mate.

White's "best" is *1* N–Q4 (to make room for his King), BxN; *2* N–B3, BxP ch; *3* K–K2. Now White has lost a Knight and Pawn, he cannot castle and his King is exposed to future attack on an *open file*. No point in continuing this one; White is better off to resign and start a new game.

There is still another class of bad positions: those in which you have developed your pieces badly, while your opponent has developed better but not enough to be able to overwhelm you quickly. Because he has developed his pieces more effectively and more aggressively, he has you under pressure. Yet, if you defend yourself successfully, you may be able to hold out.

Each time you must look for his threats; you must find ways to parry them. If possible, you must use a *developing* move for defensive purposes. Then, as you draw even with him in development, the force of his attack will diminish; the burden of your defense will become easier; you will begin to have prospects of counterattack.

This insistence on defending with developing moves is important. In Diagram 24 we have a situation in which Black is on the defensive and must choose between a developing or non-developing move.

White threatens NxBP (his Knight will be defended by his Bishop at Queen Bishop 4). This Knight move will fork Black's Queen and King Rook. Black will have to move his Queen, allowing White to play NxR with a considerable material advantage.

So much for White's threat. It is Black's move, so he has

BLACK *to play*

DIAGRAM 24

WHITE

time to defend. How? The beginner is irresistibly attracted to *1* . . . . N–K4 ? because it defends his King Bishop Pawn and also attacks White's Bishop at Queen Bishop 4. But *1* . . . . N–K4 ? is wrong because it is a *nondeveloping* move – Black is moving a piece that has already been developed.

Here is what happens: *2* NxBP !, NxN; *3* BxN ch, KxB; *4* Q–R5 ch – a fine example of the Queen's powers. (By means of this "double attack" White gives check and also attacks Black's exposed Bishop.) There follows *4* . . . . P–KN3; *5* QxB.

Black has lost his extra Pawn and the castling privilege as well. White will be able to play QxQP with a material advantage.

Now back to Diagram 24, and let's see how a more experienced player handles the situation. To defend his menaced King Bishop Pawn he plays a *developing* move, *1* . . . . N–R3 ! and he is now prepared to castle into safety.

He is also prepared for White's double attack, namely *2* NxBP, NxN; *3* BxN ch, KxB; *4* Q–R5 ch, P–KN3; *5* QxB. The same position as in the previous variation? Not at all!

For Black's Queen Knight is *developed,* guarding his Queen Pawn at Queen 5 from capture. In addition, the previous development of his King Knight now makes *5* . . . . R–K1 possible, putting this Rook into active play with the direct threat of

. . . . RxP ch. Finally, he can play . . . . K–N1 in due course, giving himself an artificial castled position and leaving his King in perfect safety.

Thus, after the second course, Black maintains material equality and a lead in development. The distinction between the nondeveloping *1* . . . . N–K4 ? and the developing *1* . . . . N–R3 ! is therefore of crucial importance. Study it repeatedly until you feel you appreciate the difference between these two lines of play.

Another good defensive technique is to ease your defensive task by seeking exchanges – the more the better. Exchanging Queens should be your particular goal, as the hostile Queen, being the most powerful piece, is usually the heart and soul of the attack. Logically, the reason for exchanging is that you will be exchanging your poorly developed pieces for your opponent's well-developed pieces. Experience shows repeatedly that judicious exchanges – value for value – are most helpful in easing the attacking menace on a hard-pressed position.

One type of defense is to be shunned – and that is *passive* defense. This is defense that is limited to parrying the immediate threat. Passive defense ignores development, counterattack, simplifying exchanges, all thoughts of a constructive future. It does not do away with the hostile threats, and, by leaving you exposed to a lasting attack, it often causes your patience or your determination to wilt.

It is not easy to illustrate this concept without going into a greatly detailed study of a complicated situation. So, suppose we examine an admittedly simplified example (Diagram 25) to grasp the basic idea.

White must move his Queen, which is under attack. He can, of course, save his Queen by thoughtlessly retreating (say by Q–N3 ?). This is good enough as far as it goes, as it does save the Queen.

But much more to the point is *1* Q–Q5 ch! with double attack

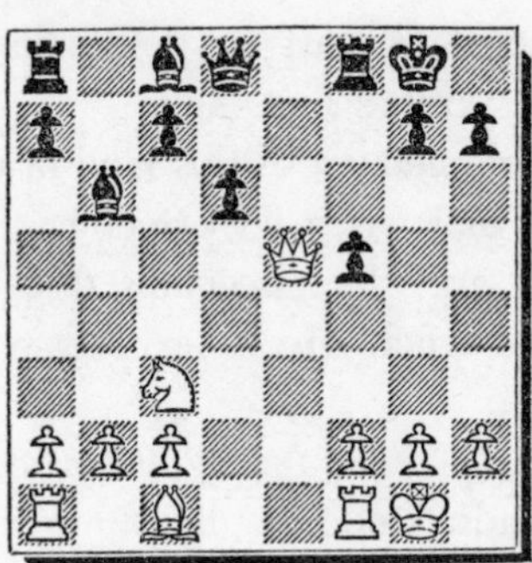

(check plus attack on Black's Queen Rook). Then, if *1* .... K–R1; *2* QxR and White has won a whole Rook. Or *1* .... B–K3; *2* QxB ch and White has won a whole Bishop.

In one case, White parries the threat – and that is all. In the second case, White parries the threat – and in so doing, wins heavy material.

And so we see that if you play the opening well, you will have good prospects in the middle game. If you play the opening badly, you will have stored up trouble for yourself in the middle game. In fact, it may well be that you have laid the cornerstone for your inevitable defeat. But more of this in the next chapter.

The value of moving first is greatly overestimated among inexperienced players. They exaggerate this value to the point where they consider it an almost winning advantage. Consequently, playing Black is an unpleasant chore which depresses them. In actual practice, White's percentage of wins is only microscopically larger than Black's.

The psychological difficulty these players face with the Black pieces is that they are under White's thumb. It is White, they say, who controls the choice of the opening. This is only a half truth, for Black has an important part in determining the opening through his reply to White's first move.

The additionally unsound complement of this kind of erroneous thinking is that when an inexperienced player has White, he overestimates his chances and then becomes discouraged when he does not achieve the quick win he expects with the White pieces.

What advantage there is in playing the White pieces may be summed up under two heads. Undoubtedly White's role is a bit more comfortable than Black's. At the start of the game, it is easier for Black to go wrong, and he must proceed with more circumspection. The second point is a related one: if Black plays the opening badly, he is likely to get into very serious trouble. If White plays the opening badly, on the other hand, his extra move may help him to escape unscathed.

The question is often asked: Does chess reveal a person's character? Indeed it does, but the revelation is not always along the same lines.

Some people reveal their character perfectly in their chess. Some are reckless, others are timid. Some are good at large-scale plans but weak in detailed execution. Some are wonderfully patient, others break loose with ill-timed projects. Some are amazingly alert, others are given to wool-gathering.

But sometimes a player's character is revealed by opposites. The player who is gifted at defense mistakenly fancies himself a great master of attack. Another player who takes the wildest risks thinks of himself as a careful, sober, patient analyst. And so the precept "Know thyself" means a great deal to a chessplayer. To the extent that he is aware of the drawbacks of his character, he can try to curb his weaknesses; and to the extent that he can do this, he will be a better player.

2. *Strategy in the Opening*

To the average player there is no, or little, distinction between strategy and tactics. Yet he will be a better player if he can perceive that distinction and turn it to account.

We might simplify considerably and say that strategy is the art of constructing advantageous situations, while tactics is the art of turning these advantageous situations into victory.

If the first explosion of the atomic bomb is considered as tactics, then all the planning, the calculations, the experiments, the interchange of knowledge, the organization of diverse skills, the stockpiling of needed materials – all these elements comprise strategy.

Which is more important? Which comes first? It is like the old riddle of the chicken and the egg. The finest strategy in the world will not bring you victory if you do not top off the strategy with forceful tactics. Tactics – checkmate, checks, captures, threats, and the like – win games. That is the theme of this book.

And such tactics are possible whether they are preceded by good strategy or no strategy at all. A powerful move is an absolute, unconditioned good. Despite this theoretical independence of tactics, it is nevertheless true that good preliminary strategy enormously heightens your opportunities for tactics. Therefore, before going on to the treatment of tactics in the main body of this book, we want to review briefly but helpfully, the main elements of good strategy in the opening.

The two basic concepts of good opening strategy are control of the center and rapid development of one's pieces.

By "the center" we mean the four squares in the center of the board: White's King 4 and Queen 4 squares, and Black's King 4 and Queen 4 squares. We measure the power of chess forces by their mobility, and both logic and experience indicate that the chessmen have their greatest power in or near the center.

(A simple example: place the Queen on one of the center squares, and she can move to 27 different squares. Place the Queen on a corner square, and she can move to only 21 squares. Try the same experiment with the Knight and Bishop, and you will reach a similar conclusion.)

In Diagram 6 we saw that a Bishop placed in the center has 13 possible moves. Compare the situation in Diagram 26.

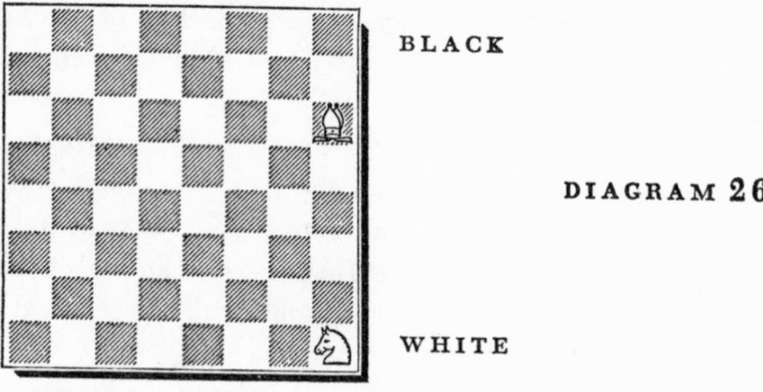

DIAGRAM 26

Here the Bishop, placed at the side of the board, has a choice of only 7 squares. Thus, we see that the Bishop placed in or near the center has much more mobility than the Bishop placed at or near the side of the board.

Similar reasoning prevails about the other pieces. In Diagram

7 the Knight had a choice of 8 squares. But in Diagram 26 the Knight, placed on a corner square, is cut down to only two moves.

From this certain conclusions can be developed.

For example, we have seen that when pieces are placed in the center, or near it, they have more mobility – more mobility than when they are placed at or near the side of the board.

Consequently it is an advantage to place your pieces in the center, or to place them where they have access to the center.

It is also an advantage to place your pieces and Pawns in such fashion that they prevent hostile pieces from having access to the center squares. In such cases, we say that your pieces and Pawns "control" the center. Should a hostile piece occupy the controlled squares, it would be captured by you. Thus your opponent's pieces are necessarily confined to the less useful squares.

In Diagram 27 we see some of the advantages of "centralized" development.

BLACK

DIAGRAM 27

WHITE *to play*

Three moves have been made by each player. What are the consequences?

White's Queen Pawn controls the important center square King 5. His King Knight has been developed to its best square – King Bishop 3 – from where it also controls the King 5 square. This is an ideal development for the King Knight.

As for White's Queen Bishop, it has been played to King Bishop 4. Here it also controls the important King 5 square, and has free diagonals in all directions. We conclude that, so far, White has developed freely and effectively.

How about Black? True, he has advanced his Queen Pawn two squares to control the King 5 square. But, by playing .... P–K3 he has neglected further control of the center. He has also blockaded his Queen Bishop, which – unlike his White opposite number – has no scope and exerts no effect on the center.

But Black has made another mistake in playing .... N–K2? (instead of .... N–KB3). This faulty Knight development has again ignored the center, and in addition it has blocked the development of Black's King Bishop.

In order to get this Bishop developed, Black will have to make another move with the Knight. Repeated moves with the same piece mean loss of time. And even after the Knight does move a second time – say .... N–N3 – this piece will still not control the important King 5 square.

The consequence is, then, that by neglecting his development and control of the center Black has laid the groundwork for a very bad, possibly lost, position.

To sum up: it is an advantage to advance your center Pawns to control center squares. For in that case, your opponent's pieces dare not occupy the controlled squares, as the pieces will be captured by your Pawns.

It is correspondingly disadvantageous if your pieces do not occupy the center; if your pieces do not command the center; if your Pawns do not control the center; if your pieces are kept away from the center by your opponent's Pawns.

The concept of developing one's pieces ties in very usefully with the idea of controlling the center. While your pieces are still on their original squares they cannot menace the enemy;

they cannot control the center; they cannot accomplish anything constructive.

Consequently, your task in the opening is to develop, and develop, and develop. Concentrate on bringing out one piece after another. Naturally, the pieces must be developed to control the center, to menace vital points in enemy territory. The inexperienced player misses the point altogether; being unfamiliar with the concept of developing the pieces, he moves the same piece again and again for lack of something better.

How operations in the center go hand in hand with effective development may be seen in Diagram 28. Here Black has a very serious problem which is often incorrectly handled by beginners.

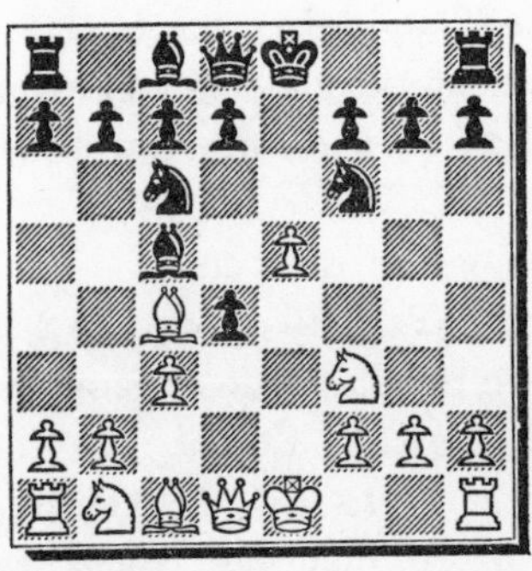

BLACK *to play*

DIAGRAM 28

WHITE

Black's King Knight is attacked by White's advanced Pawn. Naturally Black does not want to lose material. He sees that he cannot play *1* .... N–Q4 ? for then White wins a piece by 2 BxN. (Here you have an example of the way in which control of the center deprives the hostile pieces of access to the center squares.)

And Black is afraid to play *1* .... N–K5, which is answered by 2 B–Q5 or 2 Q–K2 attacking the exposed Knight and creating new troubles for Black.

So Black, by this time in a panicky mood, plays the "safe" retreat *1* .... N–KN1 ? This is bad because it negates the previous development of the Knight. Black has moved this Knight twice – only to have it end up on its original square! This is a serious loss of time that holds out discouraging prospects for Black's development.

Nor is this the end of his troubles. In order to develop this Knight, and in order to castle his King into safety, he will have to resort to .... KN–K2. Thus he will be left with a cramped game and a King Knight that has no influence on the center.

After *1* .... N–KN1? White will play *2* PxP, hitting at Black's King Bishop. Then, at the first opportunity, he will advance P–Q5, hitting at Black's other Knight and driving him off as well. White will have a sprightly initiative, strengthening his position and increasing his threats move by move – all because he has been given a free hand in the center.

But let's return to Diagram 28 and take stock of the situation once more. Black has an excellent move which will maintain his influence in the center and *thereby assure him an excellent game.*

The right move is an advance in the center: *1* .... P–Q4! In the event that White plays *2* PxN, Black replies *2* .... PxB with an even exchange of material and a good game, now that he is rid of his worries about the King Knight.

But suppose that White's reply to *1* .... P–Q4! is with a Bishop move, say, *2* B–QN5. In that case Black replies *2* .... N–K5! This is playable now, for the Knight is supported by the Black Queen Pawn. And the splendid centralized position of Black's Knight at the King 5 square is a substantial asset for Black.

To complete his preliminary development, Black can castle and bring out his Queen Bishop. Black has at least an even game, and he can face the future serenely because he has solved the problem of his King Knight in an ideal manner – by aggressive action in the center. As we saw in the previous diagram, good development and control of the center go hand in hand.

Thus, if you seek to control the center and you strive to develop your pieces, you have positive, constructive goals. The confusion is gone. And you have the encouraging feeling – quite justifiably – that you are making sound preparations for the tactical struggle to come. The better your pieces are posted, the better your opportunities for winning tactics.

There is still a further point involved that will enhance your prospects in the further play. At the beginning of the game, the King is placed in the center of the first rank. Here he is rather exposed to attack by the hostile pieces. Chess literature is full of drastic examples of what happens to a King left vulnerable in his original position.

Here is where castling comes in to save the King from a cruel fate. Note how the King is situated in the opening position (*Diagram 1*). Now review Diagrams 10 and 11 and note how, by castling, you can remove the King from the neighborhood of the centrally located pieces and tuck him away snugly near one of the corners. Once the King is in the castled position, it is much harder for the enemy to get at him.

Before we proceed, let's sum up the recommendations to this point: play out your center Pawns in order to control the center. Develop your pieces quickly and effectively. Castle early.

Before we look at some specific openings, consider another aspect of early Pawn moves in the center. These moves open up diagonals for your Bishops. If you delay or avoid such moves, you make it impossible to develop your Bishops. On the other hand, an early advance of your center Pawns makes it possible for you to develop your pieces rapidly.

To get a concrete notion of what all these theoretical considerations involve, let's briefly examine the opening moves of some of the leading lines of play.

GIUOCO PIANO

WHITE	BLACK
1 P–K4	....

White starts properly by moving a center Pawn. This gives him control of the important center square Queen 5. It also helps his development by opening the diagonal of his King Bishop. This in turn will help prepare for castling to get his King into safety.

1 .... **P–K4**

Black's advance of his King Pawn is based on the same reasoning.

Now what is White to do? To play a self-blocking move like 2 P–Q3 ? would be poor policy, as it would prevent the development of his King Bishop.

The right way is: more development. White's logical course is to bring out his King Knight – but where? If he plays 2 N–K2 he blocks his King Bishop. If he plays 2 N–KR3 the Knight has no influence on the center.

2 **N–KB3** ....

The right way. First, this move is a developing move, which is commendable. Secondly, the Knight bears on the center. Third, the move is aggressive because it attacks Black's King Pawn. Fourth, the Knight move is a preparation for castling.

2 .... **N–QB3**

A good reply. Black develops his Queen Knight and guards his King Pawn.

3 **B–B4** ....

Another good move. White develops the Bishop, controlling the important center square Queen 5 and bearing down diagonal-wise against Black's weakest point – his King Bishop 2 square. This is sound and strong development, highly recommended.

Note also that the Bishop move makes it possible for White to castle.

3 .... **B–B4**

This move is based on the same reasoning as White's previous move.

4 **N–B3** ....

White can also castle, as the squares between his King and King Rook are now empty. But there is no objection to his last move, which develops another piece. Notice that his Queen Knight also bears down on the important center square Queen 5.

4 .... **N–B3**

A good developing move based on pretty much the same reasoning as White's second move. Now Black is ready to castle too.

5 **P–Q3** ....

Once more White could have castled, but this move, opening the line for the development of his Queen Bishop, has its good points.

5 .... **P–Q3**

Black follows suit. The name Giuoco Piano is Italian for "quiet game," which is just what this opening is – a placid line often featured by symmetry. The quiet character of this opening makes it very suitable for inexperienced players.

6 Castles **B–K3**

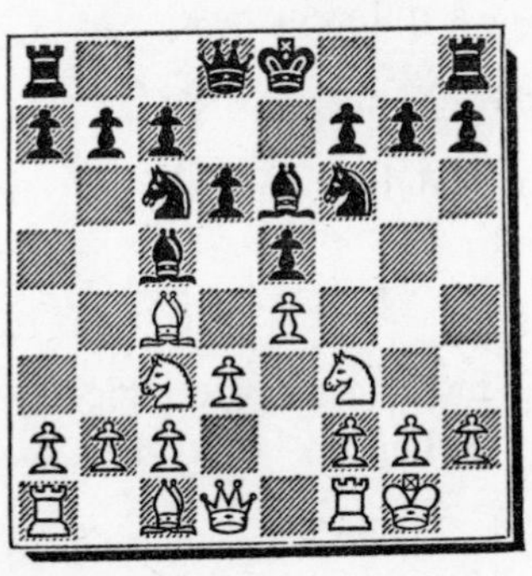

BLACK

DIAGRAM 29

WHITE *to play*

We can now take leave of the opening after observing that both sides have played on approved lines: they have advanced center Pawns, developed their pieces effectively and rapidly. White has already castled, while Black is on the point of doing so.

Both players have satisfactory prospects for the middle game because they did a good job of developing. One interesting point should be noted here. Black hopes that White will now play *7* BxB, whereupon Black, after *7* .... PxB, will have an open King Bishop file which will be occupied by his King Rook after castling.

Why is Black so eager to have the open file? Because Rooks flourish on open files. White sees the point and plays *7* B–N3. Then if Black plays *7* .... BxB White replies *8* RPxB (Pawn captures on general principles should be *toward the center*). In this form, the exchange of Bishops would give White an open Queen Rook file for *his* Queen Rook.

With these hints on strategy we leave the Giuoco Piano and turn to another opening.

FOUR KNIGHTS' GAME

WHITE	BLACK
1 **P–K4**	**P–K4**
2 **N–KB3**	**N–QB3**

These moves were explained in the previous opening comment. Now White goes off on a different tack.

3 **N–B3** ....

White develops his other Knight—not bad but not very sharp, either.

3 .... **N–B3**

Always a good developing move. Now the logical course is the development of the King Bishop on both sides.

4 **B–N5** **B–N5**

Both players are ready to castle.

But here a question arises. Can White win a Pawn by playing *5* BxN, QPxB; *6* NxP, etc.?

No, for in that case Black plays *6* .... Q–K2 (attacking White's advanced Knight). Then, after, say, *7* N–B3 Black plays *7* .... NxP, recovering his Pawn with a good game.

5 Castles   Castles

Both players have castled promptly, getting their Kings into safety.

6 **P–Q3**   ....

A significant move. White has given his King Pawn solid protection by playing P–Q3. White therefore threatens to win a Pawn by *7* BxN, QPxB; *8* NxP, etc.

6 ....   **P–Q3**

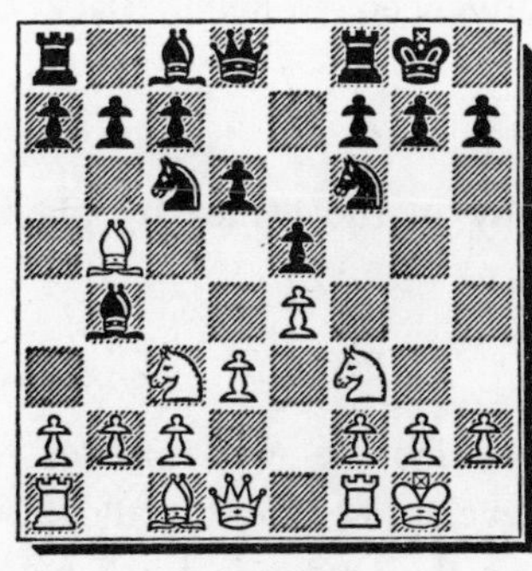

BLACK

DIAGRAM 30

WHITE *to play*

With his last move, *6* .... P–Q3, Black has solidly defended his King Pawn. Here we have a valuable point that can be applied usefully at all stages of a game. Pawn defenders are the most solid defenders because they are the cheapest and the least likely to be driven away.

The game is about even. White has a slight initiative and Black must pursue a reasonably conservative course. But both players have satisfactory prospects for the middle game.

We turn now to an opening of a somewhat more enterprising character.

PETROFF'S DEFENSE

WHITE	BLACK
1 P–K4	P–K4
2 N–KB3	. . . .

So far the same opening moves as before, but now Black gives the game a new twist.

2 . . . . N–KB3

A good developing move, to be sure, but instead of protecting his King Pawn, Black turns to counterattack against *White's* King Pawn.

After 3 NxP, Black continues 3 . . . . P–Q3 ! (attacking White's advanced Knight); *4* N–KB3, NxP with an even game. If then 5 Q–K2 (attacking Black's advanced Knight), Black defends with 5 . . . . Q–K2.

3 P–Q4 . . . .

White advances energetically in the center by playing out another center Pawn.

3 . . . . PxP

Black hopes for *4* QxP, which he will answer with *4* . . . . N–B3. This excellent developing move would also be a splendid gain of time, for since the Queen is much more valuable than the Knight, White will have to beat a hasty retreat with his Queen. (This actually happens later on.) This involves an important general principle, as we shall see.

4 P–K5 . . . .

Instead of recapturing, White interpolates an attack on Black's developed Knight. This is not what Black anticipated, and if he is rattled, he will thoughtlessly retreat his Knight

(*4* .... N–N1 ?). This kind of retrograde development is time-consuming and wasteful. Black, keeping his wits about him, therefore posts his developed Knight on an important center square.

4 .... **N–K5 !**

Well played. The Knights are ideally posted at such valuable center squares.

5 QxP ....

Now White makes the capture – and with gain of time too, as he threatens to capture Black's Knight by *6* QxN.

Naturally Black must save his Knight – but how? If he plays *5* .... N–B4 ? he saves his Knight, to be sure (since *6* QxN ?? is answered by *6* .... BxQ, and White must lose because he has given up his immensely valuable Queen for a mere Knight).

But *5* .... N–B4 ? would be the third move with this Knight out of five Black moves. Repeatedly moving the same piece is characteristic of poor players; they thereby neglect the development of other pieces.

So Black finds a better move:

5 .... **P–Q4 !**

Black defends the Knight with his Queen Pawn and at the same time opens up the diagonal of his Queen Bishop.

He also has a threat: *6* .... B–QB4, driving away White's Queen and then following up with capture of White's vulnerable King Bishop Pawn.

In this threat we again see a reason for not developing the Queen early in the game: she becomes exposed to attack by pieces of lesser value.

6 **PxP** e.p. ....

White's King Pawn captures Black's Queen Pawn in passing (see page 14). As White captures on his Queen 6 square, Black's advanced Knight is deprived of protection. Black remedies this by playing:

6 .... NxQP
7 B–Q3 ....

White develops his King Bishop preparatory to castling.

7 .... N–B3

Black develops his Knight with gain of time by attacking White's Queen – a theme that has been stressed several times.

White can save his Queen by retreating 8 Q–Q1. But this would stamp his Queen moves as complete waste of time. Therefore:

8 Q–KB4 B–K2

Black develops his King Bishop and gets ready to castle.

9 Castles Castles

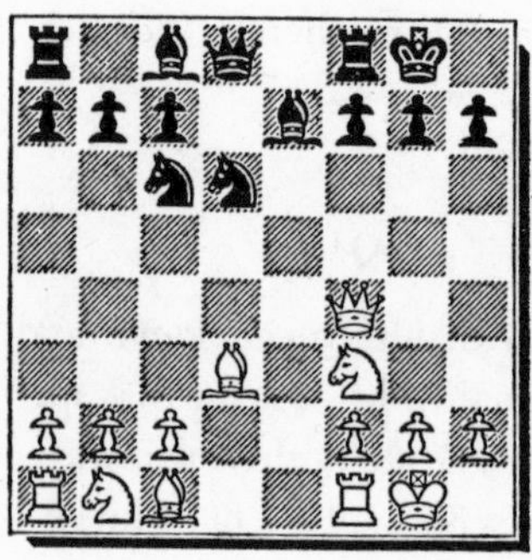

BLACK

DIAGRAM 31

WHITE *to play*

Both players have developed three pieces and both have castled – an excellent showing which leaves them with about equal prospects.

Here is an interesting facet of the play: White lost some time by moving his Queen twice. This was balanced by Black's repeated moves with his King Knight. Thus the losses of time on both sides have canceled each other out. But you must be wary of losing time by moving the same piece repeatedly when your opponent is not similarly handicapped.

Before we proceed to our study of tactics, it will be useful to see how tactics intermeshes with strategy – good strategy and bad strategy. The good strategy of the winner makes it possible for him to decide the game quickly by forceful tactics. The bad strategy of the loser exposes him to tactics against which he is defenseless.

PHILIDOR'S DEFENSE

WHITE	BLACK
1 **P–K4**	**P–K4**
2 **N–KB3**	....

So far as in previous examples. White attacks Black's King Pawn.

2 .... **P–Q3**

Black securely guards his King Pawn, but in so doing he blocks the development of his King Bishop.

3 **B–B4** ....

A good developing move which, as we know, bears down on Black's vulnerable King Bishop 2 square.

3 .... **B–N5**

A developing move, to be sure, but not a good one. Black should first develop his King-side pieces, in order to castle his King into safety.

4 **N–B3** ....

An excellent developing move which also has a devilish ulterior purpose....

4 .... **P–KR3** ??

....which Black completely overlooks. His last move contributes nothing to his development, and nothing to his King's safety. Any number of developing moves – such as *4*

.... N–KB3 or *4 ....* N–QB3 or *4 ....* B–K2 would have prevented the catastrophe that now shatters Black's game.

Black's opening strategy has been bad. But to exploit it, White must resort to tactics – brilliant, surprising, forceful, violent tactics.

5 **NxP !!** ....

If Black had seen the full strength of this amazing Queen sacrifice, he would have played the tame *5 ....* PxN, allowing *6* QxB. In that case, to be sure, White would have an easily won game, with a clear Pawn ahead and three developed pieces against no developed pieces in the Black camp. But at least Black could struggle on.

5 .... **BxQ**

Blindly he rushes to his doom.

6 **BxP** ch **K–K2**

Forced.

7 **N–Q5** mate

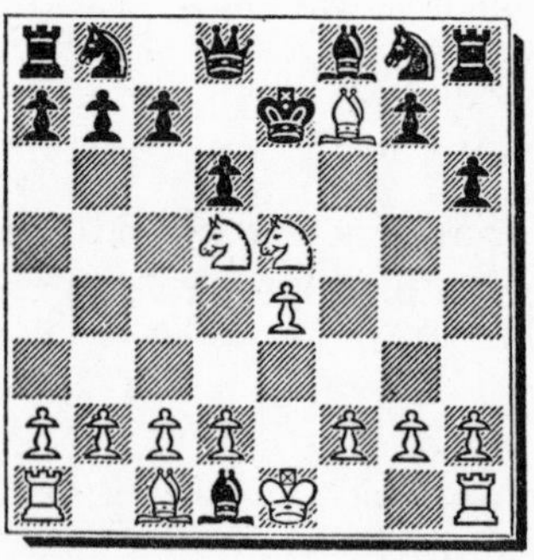

DIAGRAM 32
(*Final Position*)

Black's King is in check and has no escape. Thus in seven short moves Black has been checkmated. The reason: bad strategy on Black's part. The method: brilliant tactics on White's part.

Now for another example:

RUY LOPEZ

WHITE	BLACK
1 **P–K4**	**P–K4**
2 **N–KB3**	**N–QB3**
3 **B–N5**	....

A good development of the Bishop. White is now ready to castle.

3 .... **P–QR3**

A clever reply. In the event of *4* BxN, QPxB; *5* NxP, Black recovers his Pawn with *5* .... Q–Q5 or *5* .... Q–N4. In either case he attacks White's advanced Knight and a White Pawn.

So White bides his time.

4 **B–R4** **N–B3**

As usual, a good developing move.

5 Castles ....

Here castling not only gets White's King into safety. It also gets White's King Rook into quick play to attack Black's advanced Knight in the event he plays .... NxP.

5 .... **NxP**

This is playable, but Black's safest course is *5* .... B–K2, getting ready to castle into safety.

6 **P–Q4** **P–QN4**

Attacking White's Bishop at Queen Rook 4. Instead of retreating the Bishop, White counterattacks.

7 **P–Q5** ....

Hoping to create confusion in the enemy's ranks.

The right course for Black is *7* .... PxB; *8* PxN, P–Q3! (solidly defending his King Pawn); 9 R–K1 (attacking Black's Knight), B–B4! (defending the Knight) and Black stands well.

7 .... **N–K2**

A time-consuming retreat (avoid moving the same piece repeatedly!) which has the additional defect of blocking the development of Black's King Bishop and thus postponing Black's castling indefinitely.

8 **R–K1** ....

Bringing a new piece into the attack and gaining time by attacking Black's advanced Knight.

8 .... **N–QB4**

Black saves his Knight, but he has lost much valuable time, as he has moved this Knight three times.

9 **NxP**! **NxB**?

Black sees he can win a piece and snaps at it thoughtlessly.

10 **Q–B3**! ....

Once more we see how forceful tactics refute bad strategy. White threatens QxP mate. (Again the attack against Black's vulnerable King Bishop 2 square!)

10 .... **P–KB3**

Stops checkmate – but only momentarily.

11 **Q–R5** ch! **P–N3**

Interposing against the check – but White is relentless.

12 **NxNP**! ....

Threatening to move this Knight, uncovering a murderous check by the White Queen.

12 .... **PxN**
13 **QxP** mate!

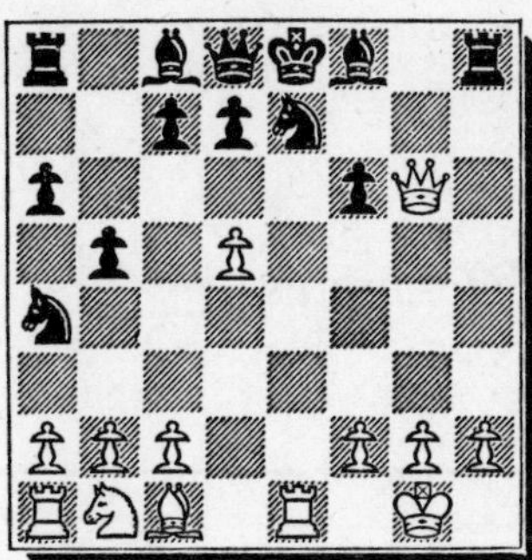

DIAGRAM 33
(*Final Position*)

This is checkmate, for Black cannot move his King out of check; he cannot interpose to the check; nor can he play . . . . NxQ, as this would uncover his King to attack by the White Rook.

In these two games we have seen how violent tactical moves force a quick decision. Such opportunities arise countless times in chess. The purpose of the following chapters is to show you how to recognize such opportunities and how to exploit them. Almost every one of the remaining diagrams illustrates a situation in which violent, forceful tactics can be applied. By studying these situations and the winning procedures used in them, you will develop the skill you need to become a good tactician in your own games. For you will become thoroughly familiar with all the powerful weapons in the arsenal of chess tactics.

3. *The Basic Checkmates*

It has been said that the great scientists are people who have "an unusual ability to get straight to the hub of the problems which fretted their minds." This ability to get right to the heart of the matter is characteristic of all statesmanship, musicianship, gamesmanship, and in fact any skill to which human beings aspire.

In chess, too, it is all-important to know what we want to achieve. This is where most chessplayers fall short. They grope and fumble *because they don't know how to win.* They don't know how to find a decisive move that may be available in any given position. They don't see their own threats. They don't see their opponent's threats. The position is just a bumbling mass of confusion to them.

The purpose of this book is to guide you to find decisive moves – to see at once the possibilities that are now hidden from you.

The key idea of this book is that constant emphasis on tactics wins games consistently. By tactics we mean such violent moves as checkmate, check, tactical tricks, captures, Pawn promotion, threats. We seek, in the next six chapters, forcing moves – violent moves – moves that impose your will on the enemy *by cutting down his choice of moves.*

The maximum forcing move is of course checkmate. This is the move that reduces your opponent's choice to zero. He has no move left: you have won the game.

In the great majority of cases you are able to force checkmate by gaining a great superiority in material. This makes it easy to enforce checkmate. In fact, a player often "resigns" – concedes his opponent's victory – when his opponent has achieved a great superiority of material.

Checkmating becomes comparatively easy when you know what are the *minimum* advantages in material you need to enforce checkmate no matter what your opponent does.

If you don't know what these minimum requirements are, you find yourself at a great disadvantage. What happens in most games is that one player heaps up an enormous advantage in material and then keeps on increasing it until he has, say, a Queen and Rook and two Bishops ahead.

Of course, to force checkmate with overwhelming material is easy. To *obtain* such an overwhelming plus, however, is very difficult, unless your opponent is much, much weaker than you.

As it happens, though, such an enormous advantage is unnecessary. You can win if you are a Queen ahead, or a Rook ahead – or, in most cases, if you are a Bishop or Knight ahead, or even a Pawn ahead! To many readers this will come as a surprise. If you're learning this for the first time, the mere information will mean a tremendous advantage in your playing strength.

To begin with, what are the minimum advantages in material you need to force checkmate no matter how your opponent plays? The following endgames are always won for the player who has the material advantage:

King and Queen vs. King
King and Rook vs. King
King and two Bishops vs. King
King, Bishop, and Knight vs. King

Let us study these one at a time.

Checkmate with the Queen

In virtually any position with King and Queen against King, the Queen should be able to force checkmate in ten moves or a little more. As in all the basic checkmates, the principle is to force the lone King to the edge of the board. Here the lone King has the least amount of mobility, and may therefore be checkmated with comparative ease.

(In each of these basic checkmates, checkmate is effected here in less than the full number of moves ordinarily required. The positions have been purposely simplified, in order to avoid getting the reader bogged down in a great deal of confusing detail.)

BLACK

DIAGRAM 34

WHITE *to play*

In Diagram 34 Black's lone King is already near the edge of the board. White therefore moves his Queen in such a way that Black's King is forced back. At the moment Black is on the point of playing .... K–B4, making a break away from the side of the board. This explains White's first move:

1 Q–N4! ....

This prevents .... K–B4 and thus forces Black's King back.

1 .... K–B2

White has forced Black's King to retreat. But now Black is ready to play .... K–B3.

2 Q–N5 ....

This prevents ....K–B3 and forces Black's King to the back rank.

2 .... **K–Q1**

With the Black King on the back rank, White has taken a big step forward. With his next move, White's Queen nails down Black's King to the back rank.

3 Q–N7 ....

Now Black's King is nailed down to the back rank. Watch how quickly White forces checkmate.

3 .... **K–K1**

Black's only move.

4 K–K6 ....

If now *4* ....K–Q1, White has 5 Q–Q7 mate or 5 Q–N8 mate.

4 .... **K–B1**
5 **Q–KB7** mate

The final position is shown in Diagram 35.

DIAGRAM 35
(*Final Position*)

Aside from the checkmating position shown in Diagram 35, the Queen can also bring about the checkmating pattern which appears in Diagram 37. (Set up the position of Diagram 37 and substitute the White Queen for the White Rook.)

Checkmate with the Rook

That the Queen can force checkmate in the ways we have described hardly comes as a surprise. For, as we know, the Queen is the strongest piece on the board. But the next strongest piece, the Rook, can also force checkmate with the aid of its own King.

The principles are the same: the lone King must be forced to the side of the board. The Rook must cut off the lone King's mobility, driving him relentlessly to one of the side rows. The Rook needs the cooperation of its own King when it comes to riding herd on the weaker King and preventing him from escaping.

Diagram 36 shows a typical situation in which we can apply these principles.

BLACK

DIAGRAM 36

WHITE *to play*

The position in Diagram 36 illustrates an important principle: when the Kings are facing each other horizontally or vertically, it is time to check with the Rook. This has the effect of chasing the lone King to the side of the board, and thus hastening the moment when checkmate will arrive.

With the Kings facing each other, White gives check:

1 **R–KB1** ch ....

The point is that Black's King is driven back to the King Knight file – one step nearer to the side of the board.

1 .... **K–N4**
2 **K–K4** ....

Note how the White King cooperates. If Black plays *2* .... K–N5, the Kings are again facing, so that White can play *3* R–KN1 ch, forcing Black's King to the side of the board.

So Black tries another way:

2 .... **K–N3**
3 **K–K5** ....

The White King stays close to the Black King to cooperate in the checkmating process.

Meanwhile, with White's Rook posted on the King Bishop file, the Black King is restricted to the King Knight file and the King Rook file.

If now *3* .... K–N2, White replies *4* K–K6. Then, if Black's King is to stay away from the side of the board he must play *4* .... K–N3, whereupon the Kings face each other. Thereupon White plays *5* R–KN1 ch, forcing Black's King to the side of the board after all.

3 .... **K–N4**

The Kings face each other, hence the Rook gives check.

4 **R–KN1** ch **K–R4**

At last the lone King has been forced to the side of the board. White must keep him on that last row – hence the Rook stays on the King Knight file until White is ready for checkmate.

In order to enforce checkmate, White needs a position in which the two Kings face each other, *with White's turn to move.*

5 **K–B4** ....

If now *5* .... K–R5, White counters with *6* R–KR1 mate. This is the characteristic mating pattern.

5 .... **K–R3**

Black's King prudently runs away; but he only succeeds in postponing mate for a few moves.

6 **K–B5** ....

And now if *6* .... K–R4; *7* R–KR1 mate.

6 .... **K–R2**
7 **K–B6** ....

More cat-and-mouse business: if now *7* .... K–R3; *8* R–KR1 mate.

7 .... **K–R1**
8 **K–B7** ....

This forces the issue: Black *must* move into the mating pattern!

8 .... **K–R2**
9 **R–KR1** mate

BLACK
WHITE

DIAGRAM 37
(*Final position*)

As we have already seen, the Queen can also checkmate in this pattern.

To sum up the situation in Diagram 37, the Rook can deliver

checkmate when (*a*) the lone King is on a side row; (*b*) the Kings face each other as in Diagram 37; (*c*) it is the stronger side's turn to move; and (*d*) the Rook can give check on the side row on which the lone King is placed.

Whereas the Queen can give checkmate from the least favorable position in about ten moves, the Rook takes about seventeen moves from the least favorable position. The difference is explained by the superior power of the Queen, which moves vertically, horizontally, and diagonally. The Rook of course does not possess this last power.

What do we mean by "the least favorable position" for checkmating? This is one in which the lone King is at the maximum distance from any side row, and the stronger side's King is at the maximum distance from the lone King.

In such cases the stronger side must spend several moves to approach the lone King. Once this approach is achieved, the King and Queen (or King and Rook) can cooperate to cut down the number of squares at the lone King's disposal, and drive him to the side of the board.

In both of the checkmating procedures that remain to be studied, the cooperation of the stronger side with his checkmating pieces is extremely instructive.

Checkmate with the two Bishops

It is impossible to force checkmate with a single Bishop. (This immediately tells us that the Bishop is weaker than the Rook.)

Each Bishop is limited to squares of one color. Consequently each Bishop is capable of occupying only half the squares on the board. Between them, however, the two Bishops are capable of occupying every square on the board. As you will see, they make up a formidable team.

First, an important limiting condition. In order to force checkmate with the Bishops, the lone King must be forced into a corner square. The process takes about the same number of moves as checkmating with the Rook.

BLACK

DIAGRAM 38

WHITE *to play*

This checkmate can be achieved systematically or it can come about after a lot of feckless drifting. What then is our plan? We intend to force Black's King to his Queen Rook 1 square and checkmate him there.

1 **B–Q4!** ....

Preventing Black's King from running away to his Queen Bishop 6 square.

1 .... **K–N5**

Black's only move. Incidentally, he attacks a Bishop.

2 **B–Q1** **K–B5**

Back again. How do we budge the Black King?

3 **B–QB2** ....

White loses time – for a purpose.

3 .... **K–N5**
4 **K–Q5** ....

The point. White's King must be right in the thick of the fight. Here he prevents another .... K–B5.

4 .... **K–N4**

He must retreat.

5 **B–QB5!** ....

This repeats the maneuver of his first move: he prevents Black's flight by way of .... K–N5. Thus White forces a new retreat on the Black King.

5 .... **K–R3**

A sorry retreat.

6 **K–B6!** ....

Note that the Kings face each other. This means that Black's King is nailed to the side row.

6 .... **K–R4**

White wants to prevent a repetition of this move, as it brings Black's King away from the mating square. White therefore repeats the time-losing maneuver of his third move.

7 **B–Q6** **K–R3**
8 **B–N4!** ....

Thus .... K–R4 has become impossible.

8 .... **K–R2**
9 **K–B7!** ....

He prevents Black's flight by .... K–N1.

9 .... **K–R3**

A brief respite.

10 **B–Q3** ch ....

White forces the Black King back. Checkmate is imminent.

10 .... **K–R2**

Black has no choice.

11 **B–QB5** ch **K–R1**

Again Black has no choice. But now his King is trapped in the fatal corner.

12 **B–K4** mate

DIAGRAM 39
(*Final position*)

Note that it is the close-in position of White's King that makes the checkmate possible by preventing the flight of Black's King.

This checkmating procedure is very instructive, and you ought to practice it until you are letter perfect in carrying it out.

Now we come to the most difficult of the elementary checkmates.

Checkmate with Bishop and Knight

This checkmate really requires skill. Some excellent players, unfamiliar with its fine points, have difficulty carrying it out. In the least favorable settings, it may take upward of thirty moves.

What makes this checkmate so laborious is that the lone King must not only be forced into a corner: he must be forced into a corner of the same color as that on which the Bishop travels.

Thus the King must be forced to a side row. Then he must be forced to a corner square of the right color.

BLACK

DIAGRAM 40

WHITE *to play*

White must force Black's King to the side, and then into a white-squared corner. (The Bishop travels on white squares.) The process will take a bit over twenty moves.

1 N–Q6 K–N3

Black stays away from his fatal Queen Rook 1 square, where the checkmate is destined to take place.

2 K–K5 ....

White's King moves in to prevent ....K–B3.

2 .... K–N2
3 B–K4 ....

And this prevents ....K–N3.

3 .... K–N1

Black has been forced to a side row!

4 K–B6 ....

He prevents Black's King from leaving the side row.

4 .... K–R1

Black still does his best to stay away from the mating square.

5 N–B7 ch K–N1
6 B–B5 ! ....

A waiting move. Black is forced to approach the mating square.

6	**K–B1**
7 **B–R7** !	....

He prevents .... K–N1.

7	**K–K1**

Now Black's King threatens to break loose with .... K–Q2. White must prevent this flight, and at the same time he must figure out a way to stop Black's King from returning indefinitely to his King Bishop 1 square.

8 **N–K5** !	**K–B1**
9 **N–Q7** ch	**K–K1**
10 **K–K6** !	....

By guarding his Knight, White forces Black's King toward the mating square.

10	**K–Q1**
11 **K–Q6**	**K–K1**
12 **B–N6** ch!	**K–Q1**
13 **B–R5**	....

Another waiting move which forces Black's King a step nearer to the mating square.

13	**K–B1**

Now it is time for White to repeat the maneuver he started on move 8.

14 **N–B5** !	**K–Q1**
15 **N–N7** ch	**K–B1**

Ir you compare Diagram 41 with Diagram 40, you can see that White has made considerable progress. Black's King has very little mobility, and has to listen to his master's voice.

16 **K–B6**	**K–N1**
17 **K–N6**	**K–B1**

DIAGRAM 41

18 B–N4 ch	K–N1
19 B–B5	K–R1

Now White has the King where he wants him, and it is merely necessary to cut off the Black King's flight to his Queen Knight 1 square.

20 N–B5!	....

The decisive maneuver.

20	K–N1
21 N–R6 ch	K–R1
22 B–K4 mate	

The teamwork of White's pieces has been very impressive.

DIAGRAM 41A
(*Final position*)

Checkmate with two Knights?

A single Knight, like a single Bishop, is unable to effect checkmate. But whereas two Bishops can force checkmate, two Knights are unable to do so.

This is one of the peculiarities of chess. Whenever the Knights corner the lone King, a stalemate * always arises. For this reason the Knights cannot force checkmate – given *best play by the weaker side.*

Strangely enough, the weaker side often loses if it has an extra Pawn. The reason for this paradox is that when the stalemate possibility arises, the weaker side can still move the Pawn, so that there can be no stalemate. (Truly an embarrassment of riches!) The two Knights are then able to force checkmate. We have a telling example of this in Diagram 42.

BLACK

DIAGRAM 42

WHITE *to play*

Black's King has been forced into a corner – first requirement for checkmate. White's King is right in the thick of things, cutting off valuable flight squares from the Black King.

Now here is our problem: in order to checkmate, we need a Knight at King Bishop 3 (to prevent . . . . K–R7), followed by

* *Checkmate* refers to positions in which a player *is in check and cannot get out of check. Stalemate* applies to positions in which a player whose turn it is to move, *is not in check and has no legal move*, and the game is a draw.

the other Knight's playing to King Knight 3 to give checkmate. (Another pattern, which you can verify, is White King at King Knight 3, and Knights at King Bishop 3 and King Bishop 2.)

But note what happens: as soon as a Knight goes to King Bishop 3, the Black King has no move and is therefore stalemated. *But, when the weaker side has a Pawn that can move, the stalemate is lifted.* That is what happens here.

1 **N–R3** ....

This Knight is headed for King Knight 3!

1 .... **K–R7**

The only move left to Black.

2 **N–N5** **K–R8**

Again the only move.

3 **N–K1** ....

The other Knight heads for King Bishop 3. Here is the critical stage. If Black replies *3* .... K–R7 we get *4* N/K1–B3 ch, K–R8; *5* N–K4. Now if Black did not have the Pawn, he would be stalemated! As matters stand, he has to play *5* .... P–Q6, whereupon White concludes with *6* N–N3 mate!

So Black tries a crafty alternative.

3 .... **P–Q6**

A gallant try. If White captures the Pawn, he can never win. But if he doesn't capture it, it will go on to the queening square! This promises to be exciting, and, as it turns out, White just barely manages to carry out his idea successfully.

4 **N/K1–B3** **P–Q7**

Once more, if White captures this Pawn, the game ends in a draw. But what else can he do?

5 **N–K4!** ....

If Black now advances his Pawn and queens it, White replies *6* N–N3 mate!

5 .... **P–Q8/N ch**

This underpromotion seems to save the day for Black, as White's King must go to King Knight 3, spoiling his intended mating pattern.

6 **K–N3** ....

BLACK *to play*

DIAGRAM 43

WHITE

Black's respite is quite temporary. As matters stand, he is preventing White from playing N–B2 mate. *But Black's Knight must move,* making the checkmate possible after all. (Such move-compulsion, where an adequately defended position collapses because of the obligation to move, is generally described by its resounding German name, *Zugzwang.*)

6 .... **N–K6**
7 **N–B2** mate

Conclusions and review

Study of these basic checkmates leads us to a valuable conclusion: when you have a certain superiority in force – a material plus, you can look forward confidently to *forcing checkmate.*

Once you have this knowledge, the game begins to make more sense to you. There is a goal, no matter how distant.

But soon you perceive a secondary goal. If you win a Pawn, you ought to be able to win the game. For, properly managed, this extra Pawn should be able to march down to the eighth rank and *become a Queen.* By obtaining such a terrific material advantage, you approach the point where you can force a fairly quick checkmate. What is more likely is that your opponent, realizing the situation is hopeless, may concede your victory by resigning.

Right now it would be somewhat premature to discuss Pawn promotion in detail. We will study it later on in its most important aspects, but here it is important to observe that much of master chess revolves about the effort to queen a Pawn. This struggle is perhaps the most common theme in master play.

In the games of ordinary players, on the other hand, the theme of Pawn promotion is sadly neglected. Consequently, once you become familiar with this vital motif, you increase your playing strength tremendously.

By way of review, it would be a good idea for you to study some of the basic checkmates by yourself; so here are some sample positions. In each case White moves first. (You can also make up your own, and practice them with a friend or by yourself.)

1. WHITE: King on King Rook 1, Queen on Queen Knight 1. BLACK: King on King 4.
2. WHITE: King on Queen Knight 7, Queen on King Rook 2. BLACK: King on King Knight 5.
3. WHITE: King on King Rook 4, Rook on Queen Knight 2. BLACK: King on Queen Bishop 6.
4. WHITE: King on Queen 2, Rook on King 3. BLACK: King on King Bishop 5.
5. WHITE: King on King Knight 6, Bishops on King 6 and King 5. BLACK: King on King 5.

6. WHITE: King on Queen Bishop 4, Bishops on King 3 and Queen Bishop 2. BLACK: King on King Knight 5.
7. WHITE: King on King Rook 1, Knight on Queen Rook 1, Bishop on King Rook 8. BLACK: King on Queen Rook 1.
8. WHITE: King on King 5, Knight on King 4, Bishop on King 3. BLACK: King on King Bishop 6.

4. *Forcing, Violent Moves*

"**Our doubts** are traitors, and make us lose the good we oft might win, by fearing to attempt."

This is a sentiment that is particularly apt in chess. When you are at a loss for a good move, you drift with the tide. You become confused; you lose heart; the game goes against you.

But, as said at the beginning of the previous chapter, you can achieve victory by finding *the forcing moves that impose your will on the enemy*. The most forcing moves of all are of course those which force checkmate.

In the last chapter we saw how checkmate can be accomplished against a lone King. Such procedures are comparatively simple. But when the board is still full of pieces, the situation is complex, and it is not easy to find the right move; or so you might think.

Yet it is in precisely such situations that a quick checkmate is feasible. It has been said that "beauty is in the eye of the beholder." Two players may be looking at the same position. One may see the right move at a glance. The other, not knowing what to look for, may never find the right move. So, we want to get an insight into the way the master's mind works.

Checks and checkmates

Every checkmate is a check, but not every check is a checkmate.

A check is by definition a powerful move: it is an attack on the hostile King. If the King cannot escape, he is checkmated – the game is over.

But even if the King can escape, the check, as we shall see, can still be very powerful. It may win material, for example. (That is what happened in the position of Diagram 14 after White's *1* RxN !)

Diagram 44 shows us why it is important to look for checks.

BLACK

DIAGRAM 44

WHITE *to play*

The trained eye immediately sees what is outstanding about this position: White's King is snugly castled and shielded by his King Knight Pawn. But the *Black* King is naked to the wind, exposed to attack in the center of the board.

There is White's target!

No need to scratch his head and wonder how to proceed. He must hound the Black King. How? By a check. And thus White's next move almost automatically suggests itself:

1 **B–B4** ch ....

This is not only check, it is checkmate! For the interaction of

White's Bishop and Queen and the Rook at King 1 cuts off any possible escape for Black's King.

Granted, this is an easy example. But the same principle applies to positions where checkmate is less obvious. Take Diagram 45 as an instance.

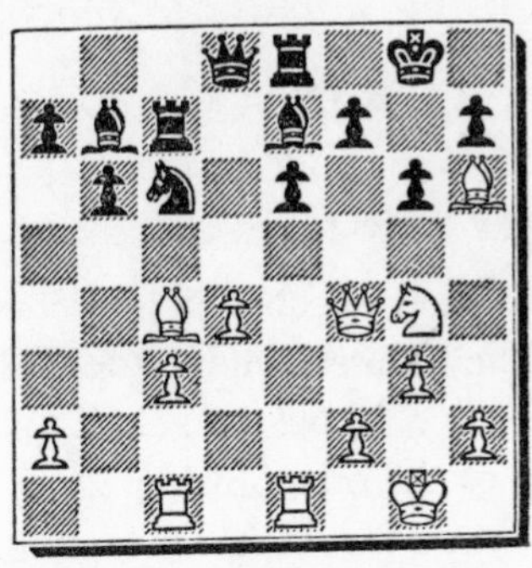

BLACK

DIAGRAM **45**

WHITE *to play*

Here, too, what strikes the eye of the trained observer is the qualitative difference in the situation of the two Kings. White's King is perfectly safe in the castled position. None of the Black forces are trained on the White King. None are near enough to threaten him.

What about the Black King? He is castled, to be sure. But note the menacing array of White pieces in the neighborhood of Black's King: White's Queen, Queen Bishop, and Knight. Even the King Bishop is on the same diagonal with Black's King, and conceivably White's Rook on King 1 might play a role in the attack.

Because of this threatening array of White pieces, the master is led to wonder whether an immediate, *violent* stroke is feasible. This reasoning leads him to play:

1 **QxP** ch!! ....

In chess terminology, this is a "sacrifice." According to our table of relative values, it is absurd to give up the Queen for a measly Pawn. But in chess, a sound sacrifice always makes sense: *you give up some material in order to achieve a greater good.* In this case, the greater good is checkmate – the highest good of all. The sacrifice of the Queen is cheap if it will result in checkmate.

What is Black to do? His King, unassisted by his colleagues, has little choice. (If *1* .... K–R1; *2* B–N7 mate or *2* Q–N7 mate.)

1 .... **KxQ**

What now?

2 **BxP** mate!

Black cannot capture this Bishop because it is protected by the White Rook at King 1. The White Knight stops him from playing .... K–B3; and as for .... K–N2 or .... K–B1, these are ruled out by the presence of the other Bishop.

The slick cooperation of White's pieces is enchanting, but it is all the product of White's expert handling of the mating attack.

IN DIAGRAM 46, now that your batting eye has been sharpened, you immediately notice that Black has two pieces, Bishop and Knight, in the neighborhood of White's King.

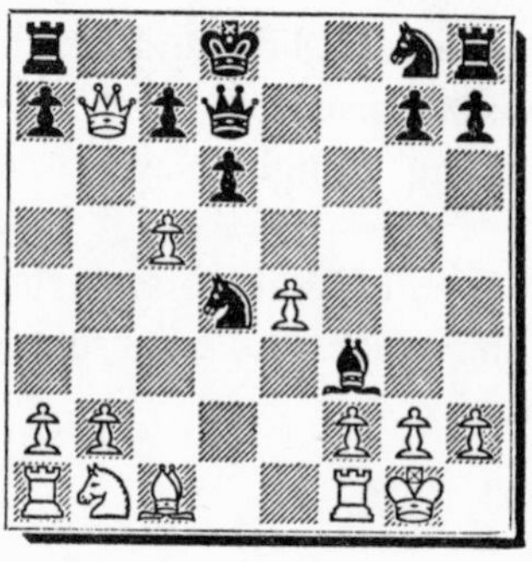

BLACK *to play*

DIAGRAM 46

WHITE

The ordinary player, at best, might notice that White's Queen is attacking Black's Rook. He might therefore take steps to protect that Rook. *But that would be too passive;* Black must look for a forcing, violent move. Actually there are two such; either way wins. Here is one:

1 .... **N–K7** ch

A forcing, violent move because it is a check.

2 **K–R1** ....

The only move.

2 .... **BxP** ch!

Another check – another forcing, violent move.

3 **KxB** ....

Again White has only one reply.

3 .... **Q–N5** ch

Another forcing, violent check.

4 **K–R1** ....

And again the only move.

4 .... **Q–B6** mate

Now for the other method. But before we examine it, note this: White has only one piece in play, his Queen. His Queen Bishop, Queen Knight, and Queen Rook are all on their home squares, doing nothing. Even his Queen is ineffective, as far as lending any support to the White King is concerned.

Where one Queen is heart and soul in the attack, and the other Queen is out of play, we have one of the important preliminaries for a devastating attack. In effect, the attacker is a Queen ahead.

1 .... **Q–N5**!

This forcing, violent move is a threat: Black menaces .... QxNP mate.

2 **QxR** ch **K–Q2**
3 **P–B6** ch ....

These checks mean nothing, because White is playing a one-piece attack.

3	K–K2
4 P–KN3	....

The only way to parry the immediate threat, but now Black forces checkmate anyway.

4	N–K7 mate

THE POSITION in Diagram 47 is deceptive, as Black is a whole Rook ahead and ought to win as a matter of course. But White has an attacking position which wrenches the game out of its normal orbit.

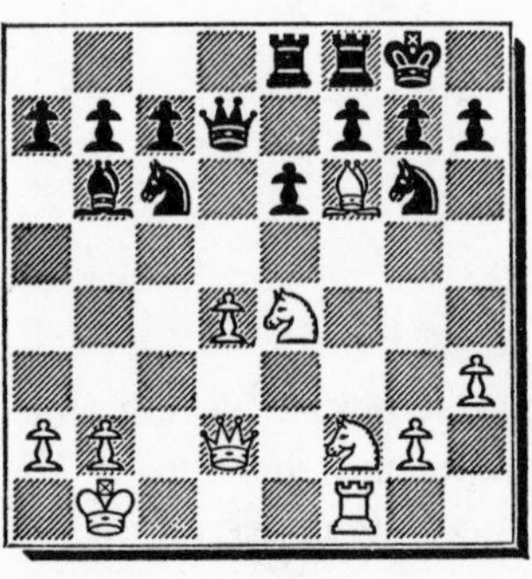

BLACK

DIAGRAM 47

WHITE *to play*

White has two pieces actively attacking: his Bishop, and his Knight at King 4. He has two more attacking units in reserve: his Queen, and his Knight at King Bishop 2.

It is Black's misfortune that his Queen can add nothing to the defense. Thus the Black King is on his own.

These considerations explain White's brilliant sacrifice.

1 Q–R6 !!	....

Threatens *2* QxNP mate, a forcing, violent move after the first forcing, violent move.

Here *1* .... PxB is refuted by *2* NxP ch, K–R1; *3* QxP mate (a useful mating pattern).

So Black plays:

1	**PxQ**
2 **N–N4 !!**	....

The point. With this forcing, violent move White threatens *3* NxP mate (another useful mating pattern) and Black has no way to stop this checkmate.

IN THE POSITION of Diagram 48, White seems to have matters all his own way, as he is three Pawns ahead and is about to win the Exchange.

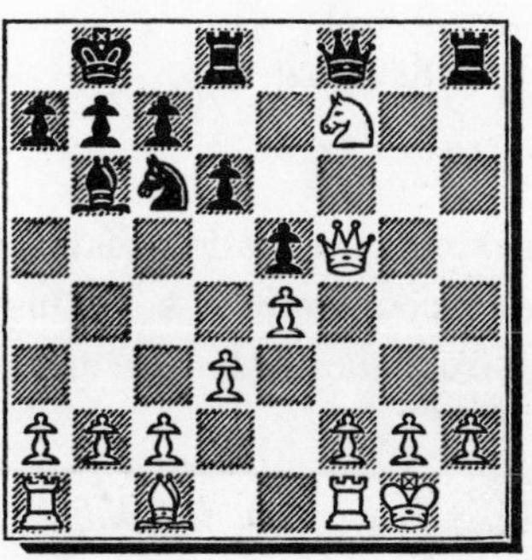

BLACK *to play*

DIAGRAM 48

WHITE

Yet the situation is not so desperate for Black as we might think. White's development has been neglected, and Black has the open King Rook file for use against White's King.

With his first move, Black prepares the setting for some glittering sacrifices.

1	**N–Q5 !**

By attacking the White Queen, Black gains priceless time for his attack.

2 **Q–B6**	....

Now White threatens QxKR or else QxQR ch. But he is completely bowled over by a startling Queen sacrifice.

2	**QxN!**

A forcing, violent move – this time a capture.

3 **QxQ**	**N–K7** ch

This and Black's next move are checks – forcing, violent moves.

4 **K–R1**	**RxP** ch!

This second sacrifice forces checkmate.

5 **KxR**	**R–R1** ch

White's King cannot flee to King Knight 1 or to King Knight 3 – thanks to Black's previous maneuver .... N–Q5–K7 ch.

6 **B–R6**	**RxB** ch
7 **Q–R5**	**RxQ** mate

IN DIAGRAM 49 we encounter a situation that is becoming familiar: three Black pieces cooperate in a mating attack while the hostile Queen is far from the scene of action.

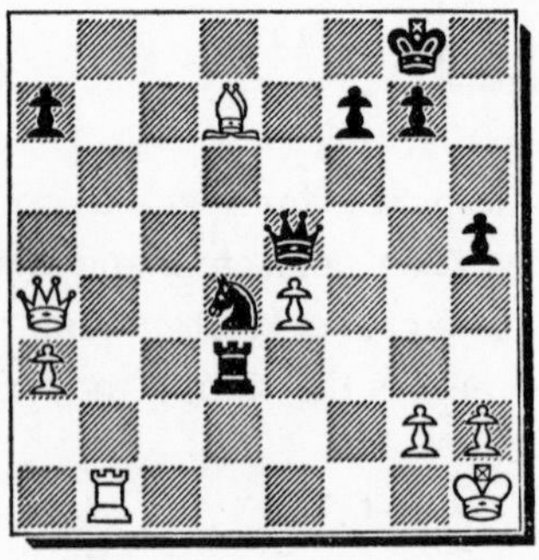

BLACK *to play*

DIAGRAM 49

WHITE

Black's Queen, Rook, and Knight are all perfectly posted to carry on a combined attack against the White King.

It is White's misfortune that he can lend no aid to his lonesome King. The White Queen is completely out of play – and we know this is often one of the indications that a contemplated attack will be successful. But the other White pieces are equally useless.

Because of these factors, Black can begin the attack with a startling sacrifice:

1 . . . . N–B6!

This threatens 2 . . . . QxRP mate. Thus Black's attack depends on one forcing, violent move after another.

If White tries 2 P–N3, Black replies with 2 . . . . R–Q7, leaving White with no defense to the deadly threat of 3 . . . . RxP mate.

So White has recourse to the obvious:

2 PxN R–Q7!

With a mating threat (3 . . . . QxRP mate) that White cannot meet. For example 4 K–N1, QxRP ch; 5 K–B1, Q–B7 mate or 5 . . . . Q–R8 mate.

Thus Black's three forcing, violent mating threats have reduced White to complete helplessness.

IN DIAGRAM 50 we have a remarkable situation which is as deceptive as it is interesting.

At first sight, we get the impression that White is irretrievably lost. His Rook at King Bishop 3 is *pinned* on the long diagonal by Black's Queen Bishop. And, since the pinned Rook has to screen White's King from attack, the Rook would have to go lost in the ordinary course of events.

Despite the depressing outlook for White's game, there is a thin sliver of hope for him. This is the fact that Black has advanced his King-side Pawns recklessly. There is a way for White to take advantage of this weakness, but the method is so subtle that only a very good player could hit on it and work it out in all its impressive detail.

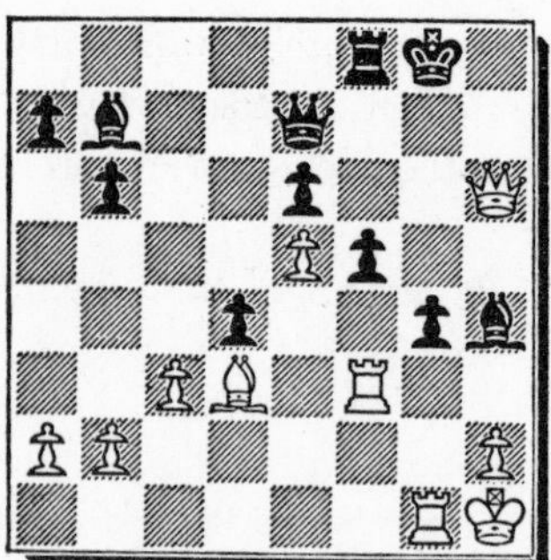

BLACK

DIAGRAM 50

WHITE *to play*

Does this mean, then, that such superb tactics are beyond the ken of the average player? Not at all.

The games of the great masters offer instructive models for us. Once we have studied, comprehended, and mastered these models, we can apply them in our own games.

One bit of valuable knowledge we do have in the position of Diagram 50: This book deals with forcing, violent moves, and if White is to save himself, it will be by some such brilliant stroke. Nothing namby-pamby can save the day.

So, here is White's brilliant inspiration:

1 **RxNP** ch!! ....

It seems incredible that this move will work, but one thing is certain: Black *must* capture the Rook. Thus White starts out with a forcing, violent move.

1 .... **PxR**

What has White accomplished?

He has opened the diagonal for his Bishop, which now plays an important role.

2 **B–R7** ch!! ....

With this beautiful point: if *2* .... QxB (giving up the protection of his Rook); *3* QxR mate.

Consequently, this forcing, violent move – this check – leaves Black with only one reply.

2 .... **K–R1**

White has achieved a great deal. He already has a draw by perpetual check: *3* B–Q3 dis ch, K–N1; *4* B–R7 ch, K–R1; *5* B–Q3 dis ch.

To achieve a draw from such a desperate setting would be creditable indeed. But White wants more – and he gets it because he has more forcing and violent checks at his command.

He has a *discovered check* in this position, by moving his Bishop. But, he says to himself, he does not want any old discovered check: he wants the most powerful, the most efficient, discovered check.

And that move is:

3 **B–K4** dis ch!! ....

This is the move that answers White's requirements. Any move of the Bishop will serve for a discovered check, *but only this one serves an additional purpose – namely, to break the power of Black's mighty Bishop on the long diagonal.*

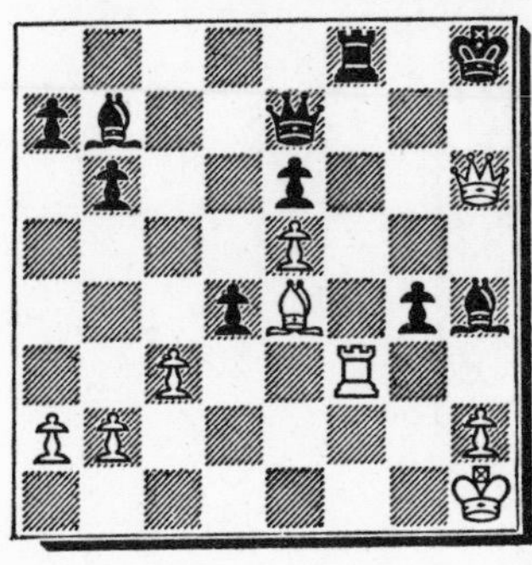

BLACK *to play*

DIAGRAM **51**

WHITE

As a result of 3 B–K4 dis ch!!, White's Rook is now unpinned, and thus *free to move.*

3 .... **K–N1**
4 **RxR** ch ....

Another forcing, violent move. Black has only one move – a move that leads directly to checkmate!

4 .... **QxR**
5 **Q–R7** mate

The final forcing, violent move that puts an end to Black's sufferings. This last example is wonderfully instructive, for it shows impressively how the search for forcing, violent moves may lead to the solution of extremely knotty problems.

All sorts of checks

So much for checkmates. But many checks are useful even when they don't lead to checkmate. For example, many checks lead to a gain of material. In other cases, a threat stands or falls because of a check.

The position in Diagram 52 offers a fine example. Black has a Bishop and Knight in return for a Rook, which, according to our table of relative values, gives him some material advantage. He hopes for an exchange of Queens, which would leave him with an excellent game.

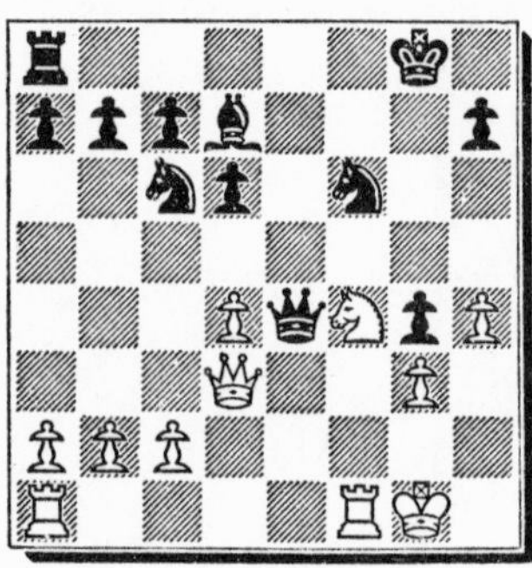

BLACK

DIAGRAM **52**

WHITE *to play*

But White is not interested in such a tame move as *1* QxQ. So he searches for a forcing move.

1 **N–R5!** ....

Who would ever dream of playing the White Knight to a square on which it is unprotected? But there is method in White's madness. Here is how he reasons:

1. Black's Queen is protected by his Knight on his King Bishop 3 square.

2. This Black Knight is unprotected.

When an unprotected piece has to guard another piece, the defender is in for trouble. The attacker's job is to hit the unprotected piece. (Here is a good example of the "overworked piece" theme treated on page 143.)

This is exactly what is accomplished with *1* N–R5 ! Black cannot reply *1* .... NxN ?? as this would lose his Queen.

But meanwhile White threatens *2* NxN ch, winning the Queen as well by depriving her of her protection. (Suppose Black had a Pawn on his King Knight 2 square, protecting his Knight on the King Bishop 3 square. In that case he could escape with a whole skin by playing *1* .... QxQ; *2* NxN ch, PxN and be none the worse for his experience. But under the given circumstances – *the unprotected state of the Knight* – White is in for trouble.)

1	**QxQ**
2 **NxN** ch	....

A forcing, violent move – a check! Black cannot run away with his Queen *because he must answer the check!*

2	**K–N2**
3 **PxQ**	....

White's forceful, violent moves have netted him a piece, so that he is now the Exchange ahead – a winning advantage in material.

DIAGRAM 53 illustrates another drastic attack on an unprotected piece – this time White's Queen. But this example is much more complicated, though not without an element of macabre humor.

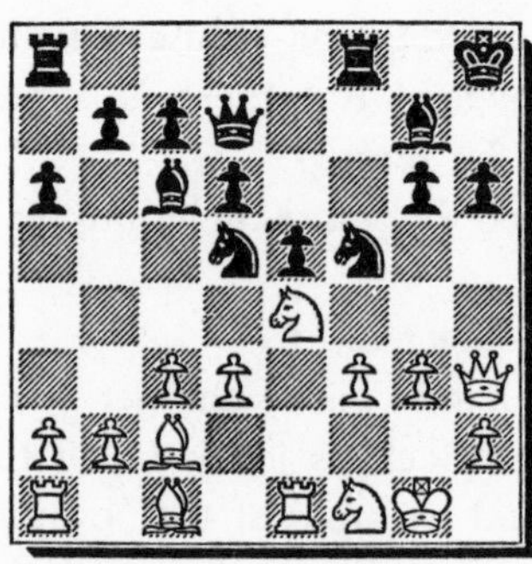

BLACK *to play*

DIAGRAM 53

WHITE

You look at this position and you ask yourself, "Where is Black's forcing, violent move?" Here is the solution: *White's Queen is unprotected.* What move can Black play to attack the Queen and attack another White unit at the same time? The answer:

1 .... N–Q5 !!

Black threatens .... QxQ as well as .... NxP ch.

This move is difficult to see because Black's Knight can be captured on its new square. However, White has no time for 2 PxN ?? because his Queen is attacked.

What is White to do? 2 Q–N2 is hopeless, as Black replies 2 .... NxKBP ch (his Knight is guarded by a Rook) followed by .... NxR.

So White captures the Black Queen.

2 QxQ ....

Now in turn it would never do for Black to play 2 .... BxQ ?, allowing 3 PxN, etc. That course would simply lose a piece.

Instead, Black must play a forcing, violent move. As we shall see later on, Black is utilizing the themes of *discovered attack* and *Knight forking check.*

2 .... NxKBP ch

And here is the required move – a check!

If White replies 3 K–N2, Black plays another forcing, violent check: 3 .... NxR ch (winning a whole Rook) and then calmly continuing with *4* .... BxQ.

3 K–R1 ....

Hoping for 3 .... BxQ, which will give him time to save his menaced Rook.

Instead, Black, with utter unconcern for the Queen, continues:

3 .... NxR !

Magnificent! Black plays another forcing, violent move, attacking a White Bishop, still keeping White's Queen under attack, and, above all, threatening *4* .... RxN mate!

4 Q–R3 ....

White does the best he can under the circumstances. He saves his Queen and protects his menaced Knight. Can it be that Black has overreached himself? No, he has still another forcing, violent move – an attack on White's Queen.

4 .... B–Q2 !

For if 5 QxB ? Black has 5 .... RxN mate – still another forcing, violent move. (White's Queen is an "overworked piece.")

BLACK

DIAGRAM 54

WHITE *to play*

White is lost:

If *5* QxB ??, RxN mate.

If *5* P–KN4, BxP !; *6* QxB, RxN ch; *7* Q–N1, RxQ ch; *8* KxR, NxB and Black is a piece and two Pawns ahead.

If *5* Q–N2, NxQ; *6* KxN and Black is the Exchange and a Pawn ahead.

SITUATIONS often arise in which a check, because of its *peremptory* nature, forces an immediate decision. This is what happens in the position of Diagram 55.

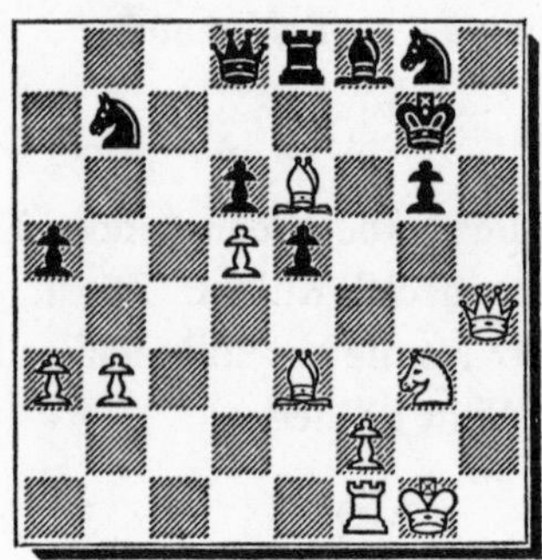

BLACK

DIAGRAM 55

WHITE *to play*

White has much the better of it, as his Queen, Knight, and two Bishops are concentrated in attack against the Black King. But in order to gain the fruits of victory, White needs a forcing, violent move. And here it is:

1 **N–B5** ch!! ....

This powerful blast clears the road to a quick checkmate.

1 .... **PxN**

White's forcing, violent move has left Black no choice.

2 **Q–N3** ch ....

Another forcing, violent check.

If now 2 .... K–B3; 3 Q–N5 mate.

2 .... **K–R2**

Or 2 .... K–R1; 3 QxN mate.

3 **QxN** mate

A PARTICULARLY vicious form of check is the discovered check. ("Discovered" here means "uncovered." A unit moves off a line and uncovers a check on that line.) Even for experienced players there is often an unpleasant sense of surprise in a discovered check, especially when the possibility has been well hidden, as in Diagram 56.

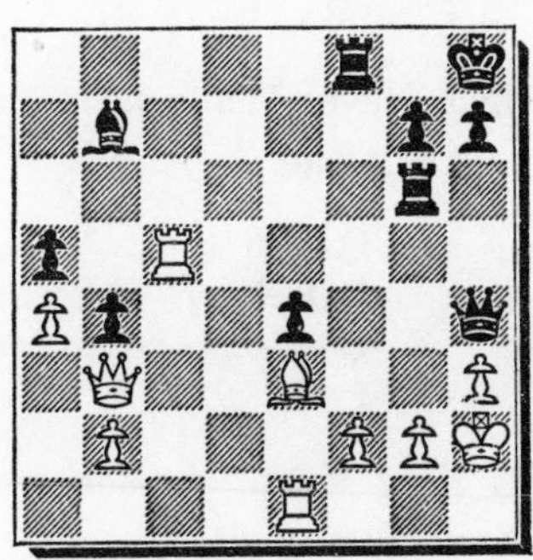

BLACK *to play*

DIAGRAM **56**

WHITE

In the eyes of most players, this position is one that is rather characterless. Black's Queen and Rooks are poised for attack on the King-side, which however seems adequately guarded by White's Bishop. Nevertheless, there is a break-through possibility for Black, based on the possibility of creating a *discovered check* for his Bishop. But how? What is required is violence of the highest order.

(There is an important hint of likely success for Black: his Queen is right on the scene of action, whereas White's Queen is idle at the other end of the board. Inactivity of the hostile

Queen always enhances the power of your violent attacks and makes them much more likely to succeed.)

1	**RxNP** ch!!

This move is obviously violent. It is also forcing, since White must capture or else be checkmated next move.

2 **KxR**	**RxP** ch!!

Another brilliant stroke. Again White must capture.

3 **BxR**	....

Another forced move. But now that the White Bishop has moved, the stage is set for a nasty *discovered check.* Black's King Pawn advances, discovering check by his Bishop.

3	**P–K6** dis ch

A forcing, violent check which leaves White little choice (*4* K–R2 or *4* K–N1 allows *4* .... QxB mate).

4 **R–Q5**	**QxB** ch
5 **K–R1**	**QxR** ch
6 **K** moves	**Q–B7** ch
7 **K–R1**	**P–K7**

Threatening to advance his King Pawn, promoting it to a Queen or Rook, and giving checkmate – a final forcing, violent stroke that compels White to resign.

IF THE DISCOVERED check is vicious, the *double check* is even more vicious. For in the latter case, what happens is that the piece which steps aside to open up the line of check also gives check! This means that the victim cannot interpose on either checking line, nor can he capture either checking piece.

So the victim has only one way of answering the check – by moving his King. With his defensive resources so circumscribed, his chances of resistance are meager indeed. In fact, the mortality rate from double checks is very high: they often force checkmate. In any event, they rank in the very forefront of forcing, violent moves.

Black's procedure in the set-up of Diagram 57 gives us some idea of the bombshell technique of the double check.

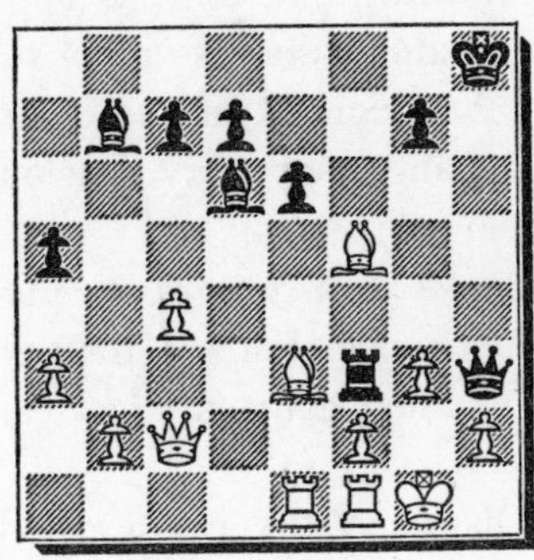

BLACK *to play*

DIAGRAM 57

WHITE

An experienced player, confronted with this position, would immediately pay his respects to Black's Queen Bishop reaching greedily along the long diagonal into the heart of White's castled position.

Even so, he might go wrong with *1* .... RxNP ch?? expecting *2* RPxR ??, Q–R8 mate (or *2* .... Q–N7 mate). For White would reply *2* BPxR !!, creating a defense by his Queen along the second rank against the possibility of .... Q–N7 mate.

The trouble with *1* .... RxNP ch?? is that it is not forcing and violent enough. We need madder music. Here is the move that does the trick:

1 .... **Q–N7** ch!!

No doubt about it: White has only one reply.

2 **KxQ** **RxNP** mate!

Black is giving *double check.* White cannot interpose to the Bishop's attack because the Rook continues to check. Nor can White capture the Rook because the Bishop continues to check.

And 3 KxR is impossible because the Rook is protected by the Black Bishop at the Queen 3 square. Thus White has no escape.

Captures and exchanges

Exchanging pieces (capturing one of your opponent's men for one of your own of the same value) is one of the most frequent – and most prosaic – happenings on the chessboard. Yet many a harmless-looking exchange may carry a vicious sting in its tail.

In this sense, *a capture which forces a capture in return* may be revealed as a forcing, violent move. For the forced recapture may set the stage for a winning coup, a check, or some other forcing move.

The winning procedure in Diagram 58 is a typically demure example of the deadly consequences that may result from a "simple" exchange.

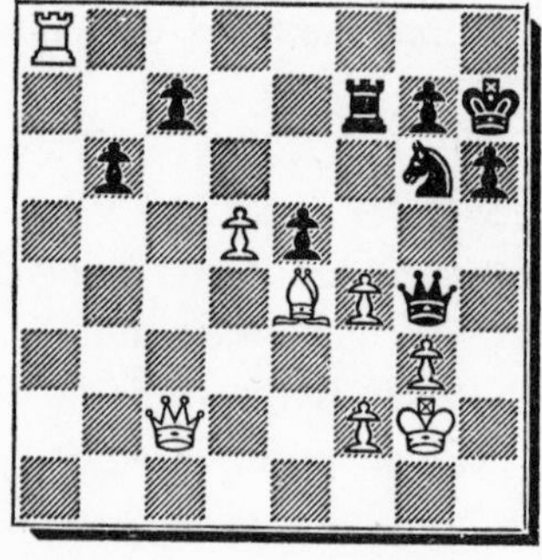

BLACK

DIAGRAM 58

WHITE *to play*

White begins with a forcing, violent, capturing check which leaves Black with no choice:

1 BxN ch ....

Black has only one reply.

1 .... QxB

Thus Black maintains the balance of forces – not that he has any alternative.

2 **R–R8** ch! ....

But this is ruinous for Black. He *must* capture the Rook – and consequently loses his Queen.

2 .... **KxR**

Black's King is an "overworked piece." He cannot continue to protect his Queen.

3 **QxQ** ....

And White's material advantage gives him an easy win.

SOMETIMES a capture that wins material is based on the foreseen resource of a check or other forcing, violent move that saves the day. That is what happens in the position of Diagram 59. Black sees that he can win a Pawn, despite what seems like a perfectly adequate resource on White's part.

BLACK *to play*

DIAGRAM 59

WHITE

Black starts the sequence with a forcing, violent move – a capture.

1 .... **NxP!**

So that if 2 NxN, RxN, and Black has won a Pawn. White sees this, and thinks he can cross Black's intentions with a forcing, violent move of his own – another capture.

2 NxB ....

Expecting 2 .... RxN? which he will answer with 3 NxN, which leaves White with a piece to the good and a won game. Instead:

2 .... **NxN ch!**

A forcing, violent, capturing check which enables Black to avoid the loss of a piece.

3 PxN **QRxN**

Thus Black has achieved his objective: winning a Pawn. This should win the game for him.

IN DIAGRAM 60 we again encounter a position in which a forcing, violent check leads to an exchange which in turn provides the setting for a forcing, violent move that wins material.

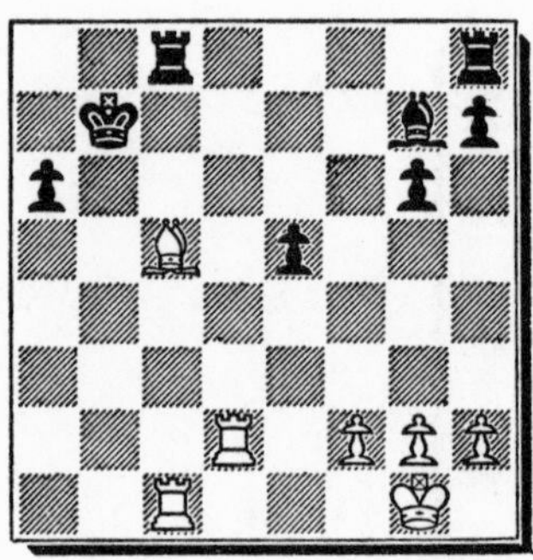

BLACK

DIAGRAM 60

WHITE *to play*

Since White is a Pawn down, he must do something forceful if he is to stave off ultimate defeat.

1 **R–Q7 ch!** ....

A forcing, violent check that threatens to win Black's Bishop (*double attack*) and leaves Black with only one reply:

1 .... R–B2
2 RxR ch ....

Again he leaves Black with no choice.

2 .... KxR

And here is the crisis: White has a *discovered check* by moving his Bishop. There is only one correct move. Which is it?

3 B–B8 dis ch ....

A violent forcing move. He gives check and simultaneously attacks Black's Bishop. Black must move his King out of check, allowing White to continue *4* BxB, with a piece up and an easy win.

MANY A TACTICAL finesse hinges on a check, or some similar unexpected forcing move that can ruin even the most careful calculation. This is exemplified in the play from Diagram 61. Black thinks he can win a Pawn; White disagrees.

BLACK *to play*

DIAGRAM 61

WHITE

Black's idea is to cut off White's Pawn protection of White's advanced Knight at the King Bishop 5 square.

1 .... NxKP ?!

Obviously White cannot reply 2 QxN ? as this would lose the Queen.

And if *2* NxN? Black replies *2* .... QxN, having won the Pawn as planned.

2 **RxN!** **QxN**

So far, so good. Black has won the Pawn.

3 **RxR** ....

Attacking Black's *unprotected* Queen. But Black has foreseen this move, and is prepared for it.

3 .... **QxQ**

Anticipating *4* PxQ, RxR and Black retains his Pawn advantage.

But now comes a *check* – a forcing, violent move that Black has completely overlooked.

4 **RxB** ch! **KxR**

Any other capture leads to the same result.

5 **PxQ** ....

Thanks to his surprising fourth move, White has won a piece.

And the moral? When you calculate a sequence of moves, you must make sure that the sequence is foolproof. At any point the sequence may be shattered by the interpolation of a forcing, violent move that leads to a disastrous change in your plans.

ON THE OTHER HAND, many an exchange sequence depends on a long-foreseen tactical benefit.

This is shown to good advantage in Diagram 62. White starts a drastic simplifying maneuver based on the existence of his passed Rook Pawn.*

* A passed Pawn is a Pawn whose advance is not impeded by hostile Pawns. In this case, White's Queen Rook Pawn is passed because Black has no Queen Rook Pawn and no Queen Knight Pawn. Such a Pawn is well on the way to becoming a Queen by advancing to the last rank. It is therefore a powerful weapon.

If White plays *1* BxB, QxB; *2* P–R7 (threatening to queen the passed Pawn), Black holds everything with *2* .... R–B1.

White realizes, then, that he needs something more forcing in order to turn his passed Pawn to account.

Before White embarks on any radical departure from this position, he must take account of the material relationship. Right now he has a Rook and Pawn for two Knights. This is slightly in White's favor; and of course the passed Pawn has great dynamic power.

1 **QxR!** ....

A forcing, violent move. Black's reply, which opens the King Knight file, is forced.

1 .... **PxQ**

Now White must justify his brilliant sacrifice.

2 **RxB** ch ....

A forcing, violent check. Now Black's Queen also disappears.

2 .... **QxR**
3 **BxQ** ....

In view of what happens after Black's next move, he can now try *3* .... NxP in order to get rid of White's formidable passed Pawn. But in that case White replies *4* BxN, with a whole Rook ahead and an easy win in prospect.

3 .... **KxB**

Now White has a forcing, violent move against which Black is completely helpless.

4 P–R7 ....

And wins. No matter how Black plays, White advances the Pawn to the eighth rank and promotes it to a Queen, thus gaining an enormous material advantage.

The whole line of play from Diagram 62 is extremely instructive. Play it over several times until you are sure you understand the basic idea and all its contributory details. That basic idea, to recapitulate, is to simplify the position by a number of forcing captures in order to make it impossible for Black to stop the passed Pawn from queening.

Pawn promotion

The last example turns our attention to one of the most powerful themes in the realm of forcing, violent moves. This is the theme of Pawn promotion.

Few features of the game of chess are so neglected as the theme of Pawn promotion. Though the Pawn is the lowliest of all the chessmen, its potential power of being converted into a piece by promotion greatly increases its value.

The average player places little importance on the gain or loss of a Pawn, because he is unaware of the techniques of bringing a Pawn to the queening square. There are, practically speaking, two aspects of the Pawn's power.

1. If it queens unimpeded, the player who promotes the Pawn is a whole Queen ahead. This should decide the game for him in short order.

2. If the defender can give up a piece for the new Queen and the attacker can capture this piece, the attacker has won a piece. This too should win the game for him.

Ponder these propositions well. The play in the following diagrams will clarify them for you.

AS WE KNOW from the first chapter, a lone Bishop cannot force checkmate. The position of Diagram 63 is extremely instructive. *White can win because he has one Pawn left.* In order to win, he must (*a*) win Black's remaining Pawn; (*b*) advance his Pawn to the queening square. Black cannot prevent White from obtaining a new Queen. This brings home the idea that Pawn promotion is a forcing, violent move.

BLACK

DIAGRAM 63

WHITE *to play*

White begins by attacking the Black Pawn.

1 K–Q7	....

Black can no longer defend his Pawn.

1	K–R3
2 KxP	K–R2
3 K–Q8	K–N1
4 P–B7 ch	K–R2
5 P–B8/Q	....

And now, with a Queen and Bishop to the good, White wins with ease.

SOMETIMES the defender is able to capture the queening Pawn and then loses the capturing piece. Here too the attacker almost invariably wins, once more demonstrating that Pawn promotion is a forcing, violent move. Diagram 64 is a case in point.

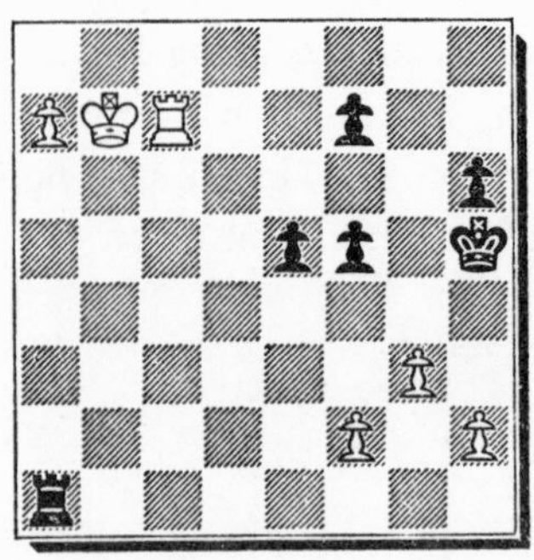

BLACK *to play*

DIAGRAM 64

WHITE

White is on the point of queening his far-advanced Rook Pawn. Black desperately tries to keep on checking, in the hope of preventing the Pawn from queening.

1 .... **R–QN8** ch

Now if White plays *2* K–R8, he blocks the advance of his Rook Pawn.

2 **K–B8** ....

Threatening to queen the Pawn.

2 .... **R–QR8**

Momentarily preventing the Pawn from queening.

3 **K–N8 !** ....

Threatening *4* P–R8/Q, RxQ ch; *5* KxR and White has won a Rook with an easy victory in sight. (The superiority of *3* K–N8 ! over *3* K–N7 will become clear in the next note.)

3 .... **R–QN8** ch
4 **R–N7 !** ....

The point. Now that White has interposed with the Rook, his King can no longer be harried by checks. Meanwhile the Pawn again threatens to queen.

4	R–QR8
5 P–R8/Q	RxQ
6 KxR	....

With a Rook ahead, White has an easy win.

CONNECTED passed Pawns are even more formidable than a single passed Pawn. For one thing, they threaten to convert into two Queens. Another point to remember is that such Pawns can protect each other. Their power is shown in the play from Diagram 65. At once we can appreciate the forcing, violent nature of Pawn promotion.

BLACK

DIAGRAM 65

WHITE *to play*

White is the Exchange down, but this does not signify in view of the fearful power of his cluster of passed Pawns.

1 P–K7	K–B2

If *1* .... R/B4–B1; *2* P–Q7 is crushing, for then White attacks a Rook and simultaneously threatens to queen in two different ways.

2 P–Q7	....

Black resigns. He is helpless against the coming *3* P–K8/Q ch or *3* P–Q8/Q.

In the last three examples we have seen the enormous power

of Pawn promotion. Such promotion, when it is successful, reduces the opponent to utter helplessness.

IN DIAGRAM 66, too, we see the forcing, violent power that is unleashed by a queening Pawn.

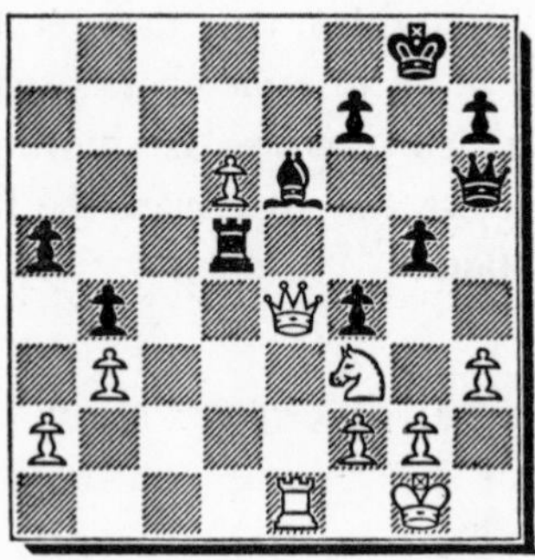

BLACK

DIAGRAM 66

WHITE *to play*

White has a passed Queen Pawn that seems predestined to queen. But it cannot advance at once, of course, for then Black simply replies .... RxP.

White wins by a forcing, violent move – a capture.

1 **QxR!** ....

White gives up his Queen, as he will soon get a new one.

1 .... **BxQ**
2 **R–K8** ch ....

If now *2* .... Q–B1, it would be a great blunder to play 3 RxQ ch?, KxR; *4* P–Q7 because of *4* .... K–K2 and Black wins the passed Pawn.

Instead, on *2* .... Q–B1 White plays 3 P–Q7! (a characteristic queening procedure). Now if Black stands pat, White continues with *4* P–Q8/Q, with an enormous material advantage which wins easily.

On the other hand, after *2* .... Q–B1; *3* P–Q7, it does Black no good to play *3* .... QxR, as White replies *4* PxR/Q ch, likewise winning easily.

2	K–N2
3 P–Q7	Q–Q3
4 P–Q8/Q	....

With the advantage of a Rook ahead (after *4* .... QxQ; *5* RxQ), White wins without any trouble.

BECAUSE the promotion of a Pawn is so powerful, it often becomes possible to play strikingly brilliant sacrifices to ensure the queening of a Pawn.

In Diagram 67 White is the Exchange ahead for two Pawns. But Black's passed Pawns are no menace, whereas White's passed Queen Pawn is a real threat.

BLACK

DIAGRAM 67

WHITE *to play*

As usual, forcing, violent moves are the key to the situation.

1 RxB !	....

A forcing, violent move. This capture sacrifices the Exchange *in order to draw Black's Queen away from the defense.*

1	QxR
2 QxR ch!	....

Another forcing, violent move – this time a capturing check.

2	NxQ
3 P–Q7!	....

A quiet move – but what power! The Pawn threatens to queen *in two different ways*. This leaves Black helpless, for example 3 .... Q–B7; 4 P–Q8/Q ch or 3 .... Q–Q7; 4 PxN/Q ch. In either event, White's material plus is overwhelming.

SOMETIMES the queening of a Pawn has to be accomplished with delicate timing. This is admirably illustrated in Diagram 68.

BLACK *to play*

DIAGRAM 68

WHITE

Unlike the previous position, this one is greatly simplified. Nonetheless, Black's passed Queen Bishop Pawn is a mighty power. Momentarily White's Bishop prevents the Pawn from advancing. What can Black do about it?

1	P–K5 ch!

A forcing, violent move – a Pawn check that attacks White's King and Bishop simultaneously, and thus forces White's hand.

2 BxP	....

Or 2 K–K3, PxB; 3 KxP, N–Q4 and Black wins easily.

2	**NxB**
3 **KxN**	**P–B7**

And Black's passed Pawn must queen.

SO FAR we have had a good insight into the peremptory nature of forcing, violent moves. We can now understand how, in game after game, moves of this powerful nature make it possible for us to win – and win by effective, purposeful play.

But there are other tactical tricks that will help you win many a game. They are easily mastered, and of quite common occurence. So let us turn to the next chapter to perfect our skill in the use of these weapons.

POSITIONS FOR FURTHER STUDY

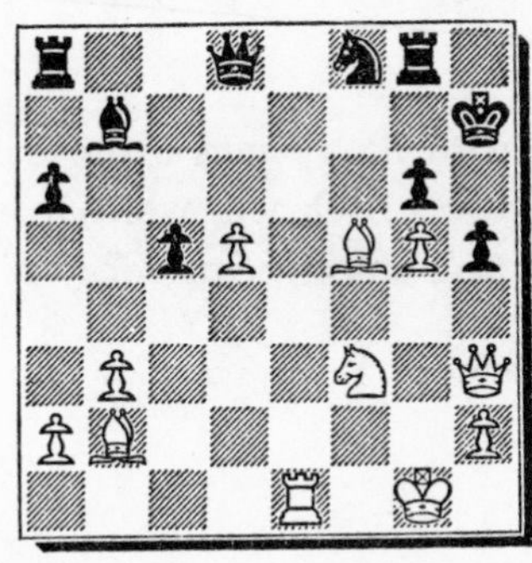

BLACK

DIAGRAM 69

WHITE *to play*

White has a menacing attacking position, especially in view of the powerful action of his Bishops. What is the most effective way for him to proceed?

BLACK *to play*

DIAGRAM 70

WHITE

Black is the Exchange ahead, so there is no doubt of his ultimate victory. Is there any way for him to win quickly?

BLACK

DIAGRAM 71

WHITE *to play*

This is an exciting position, with both Kings exposed to attack. Obviously White must move his Queen, which is under attack. What would be the Queen's *strongest* move?

BLACK

DIAGRAM 72

WHITE *to play*

Black's pieces are ineffectually bunched together. If White is alert to his opportunities, he can exploit the situation relentlessly. What would you suggest?

5. *Winning Tactical Tricks*

To the uninitiated player, a forceful winning move seems to be the product of intuition or some other mysterious source. This makes chess very interesting but also very tantalizing.

But if we look at a great many winning moves, the mystery vanishes quickly enough. These winning moves can all be classified into clearly defined groups. We can take these groups, analyze the basic mechanism underlying each one, *and then apply the principles in our own games.*

In this chapter, then, we shall consider the most common of these powerful tactical tricks. Once you have studied the following examples, you will be ready to apply these methods and thus win many more games than you have in the past.

The pin

The pin is perhaps the most frequent of all the common tactical tricks.

Just what is a pin?

A pin is an attack on a hostile piece *which cannot move because it screens a second piece from attack.*

The piece which does the pinning is called the *pinning piece.*

The piece which is under pressure not to move is called *the pinned piece.*

The piece which is guarded from attack is called *the screened piece.*

The pinning attack can take place on a rank, a file, or a diagonal.

Since it is not easy to visualize these terms, let us see how the pin operates in a real game.

BLACK

DIAGRAM 73

WHITE *to play*

White has a very superior position, and the Black Queen is badly out of play. Actually White can decide the game at once by a forcing, violent move:

1 **Q–B6** mate! ....

On being told that this is checkmate, we rub our eyes in amazement. But then we see that Black cannot play *1* .... PxQ because his King Knight Pawn is *pinned.* It cannot move, for to do so would expose the Black King to attack by White's Bishop.

(Such a pin, in which the screened piece is the King, is called an *absolute pin.*)

TIME and again you can win valuable material by means of a pin. This exceedingly practical hint is effectively illustrated in Diagram 74.

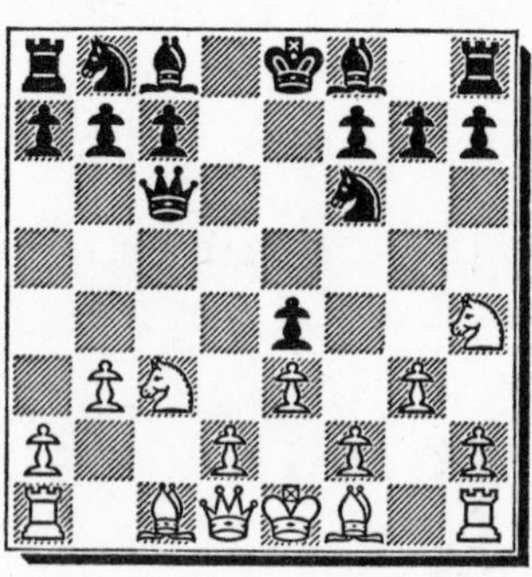

BLACK

DIAGRAM 74

WHITE *to play*

As you study this position, you can see how enormously your playing strength is increased if you are familiar with pinning technique. If the subject is a closed book to you, then the position is puzzling. All sorts of moves might be played here, and it is laborious as well as cumbersome to try to decide which move is advisable.

But if you know about the pin, *you immediately hit on the forcing, violent move that is by far the strongest in the situation:*

1 **B–N5!** ....

After this crushing stroke, Black might just as well resign on the spot. Why?

White's Bishop at Queen Knight 5 pins Black's unfortunate Queen, which is on the same diagonal with Black's King. Because the Black Queen screens the King from attack, the Queen cannot run away. Finally, White's Bishop at Queen Knight 5 is guarded by White's Knight at Queen Bishop 3.

Add up all these facts and you see that White wins the Black Queen in return for a mere Bishop. This is such a huge material advantage that there is no point in Black's playing on.

IN DIAGRAM 75 we have a much more subtle example, because it involves two possible pins. However, this twofold aspect of the position makes it extremely instructive because it adds that much more to our understanding of the insidious way that the pin works.

BLACK

DIAGRAM 75

WHITE *to play*

What makes the solution of our problem difficult is that no pin exists right now. *White must create a pin.* The piece which will do the pinning is either the White Bishop at Queen Knight 3, or else the White Queen. White begins with a capture (a forcing, violent move):

1 **NxB!** ....

Black can retake in one of two ways. If he plays *1* ....PxN, there follows 2 RxN! winning a whole piece as Black's Queen Pawn is pinned by White's Queen. (If 2 ....PxR; 3 QxQ with an overwhelming plus for White.)

1 .... **QxN**

Black recaptures the other way, but disaster overtakes him just the same.

2 **RxN!** ....

Again White wins a piece, for this time Black's Queen Pawn

is pinned by White's Bishop at Queen Knight 3. (If *2* .... PxR; *3* BxQ, again with an overwhelming plus for White.)

IN DIAGRAM 76 it is almost certain that a player unfamiliar with the pin would never even dream of the winning move, which almost involves sleight of hand!

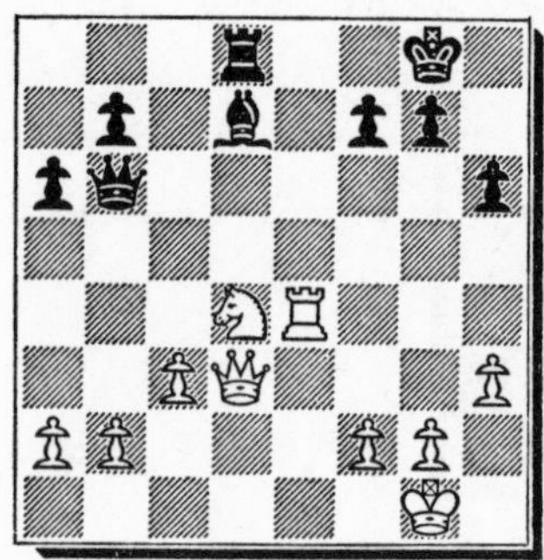

BLACK *to play*

DIAGRAM 76

WHITE

What adds to the piquancy of the winning maneuver in this position is that in the actual game a great master playing the Black pieces failed to find the right move!

To win, Black must move his Bishop to a square on which it is unprotected. Instinctively we shrink from such a move, but in this case we must overcome our aversion. Black's winning move is forcing and violent:

1 .... **B–B4!**

White can reply *2* NxB, to be sure, but in that case he loses his Queen: *2* .... RxQ etc. In other words, White's Knight is pinned by Black's Rook. (This is a *relative pin.* Since the screened piece – White's Queen – is not the King, White can legally expose the screened piece to attack. But this involves such a severe loss of material that for all intents and purposes we can speak of *2* NxB as being "impossible.")

However, there is more to this position. After *1* .... B–B4!

Black pins White's Rook, which screens White's Queen from attack. A move of White's Rook would lose his Queen for a mere Bishop – a crushing loss of material for White. Consequently White must leave his Rook where it is, losing it in return for the Bishop. This is "losing the Exchange" – see page 20 – signifying a loss of material that should cost White the game.

IN DIAGRAM 77 we find an amazing situation: White, subjected to an apparently murderous pin, nevertheless escapes unscathed – and actually wins! The wherefore of his narrow escape is fascinating.

BLACK

DIAGRAM 77

WHITE *to play*

Many players with the White pieces would find this predicament so depressing that they would resign at once. Black's Rook on Queen Bishop 7, protected by his Queen, pins White's Queen. The unlucky White Queen is trapped as she screens White's King and therefore must not move.

Yet White has a sly resource which wins for him – a *counter-pin!*

1 **R–QB1** !! ....

This powerful resource is so forcing and so violent that it cancels out the power of Black's pin.

The point is that Black cannot capture White's Queen because of the counterpin on the Black Rook, which has the duty of screening Black's King from attack. Now that this Rook is doubly attacked, Black has nothing better than *1* .... RxR, allowing the easily winning reply 2 QxQ.

Suppose the Queen Bishop file were not open; for example, assume that Black had a Pawn on his Queen Bishop 2 square. In that case, *1* R–QB1 would be a ghastly blunder, *as the Black Rook would not be pinned* and Black could simply play *1* .... RxQ ch.

Or imagine that Black's Queen were guarded by a Black Pawn at Queen Knight 6. In that case, even if the Queen Bishop file were open, *1* R–QB1 would still be disastrous, as after *1* .... RxR; 2 QxQ, Black would simply play 2 .... PxQ.

In other words, the finesse in Diagram 77 becomes operative because the Queen Bishop file is open – allowing White to paralyze the action of the pinning Rook – and because Black's Queen is *unprotected.*

THIS LATTER theme – the unguarded screened piece – is also admirably illustrated in Diagram 78.

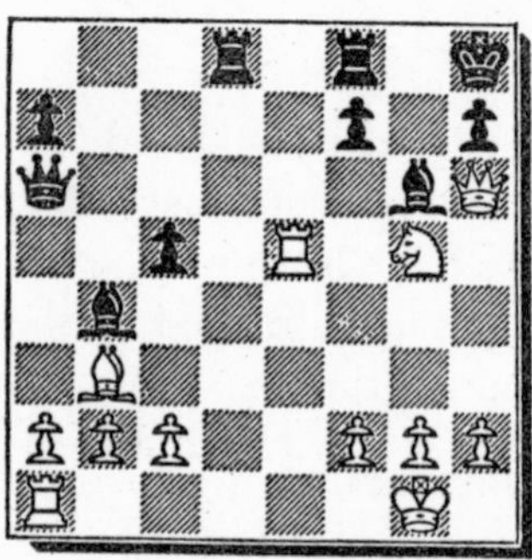

BLACK

DIAGRAM 78

WHITE *to play*

Here we have another position in which familiarity with basic attacking themes enables us to find our way through a maze of possibilities.

White has his pieces concentrated for the most part on the King side. Black's King is vulnerable, and his Queen is out of play at the other side of the board.

White's winning attack is based on the fact that *Black's Queen is unprotected.*

1 NxRP! ....

A forcing, violent capture that threatens 2 N–B6 dis ch, followed by mate next move.

Note that Black cannot play 1 .... BxN, in view of the winning reply 3 QxQ. Black's Bishop is *pinned.*

1 .... **B–Q7**

A clever attempt at diversion. Black optimistically hopes for 2 Q–R4, BxN – when he can draw a breath of relief.

2 N–N5 dis ch! ....

White refuses to be diverted. This forcing, violent discovered check leaves Black with only one reply.

2 .... **K–N1**
3 R–K6! ....

Another forcing, violent move.

If now 3 .... PxR; 4 QxB ch, K–R1; 5 Q–R7 mate.

If 3 .... BxN; 4 RxB ch!, QxR; 5 QxQ ch and wins – Black's King Bishop Pawn is *pinned* by the White Bishop. These are beautiful, instructive possibilities.

3 .... **QxR**

If Black's Queen runs away, White replies 4 RxB mate! (Note again that Black's King Bishop Pawn is pinned by White's Bishop.)

4 BxQ **Resigns**

With only a Rook for a Queen and with White's attack still functioning powerfully, Black sees that his situation is hopeless.

IN DIAGRAM 79 our knowledge of pinning techniques guides us to a brilliant winning method.

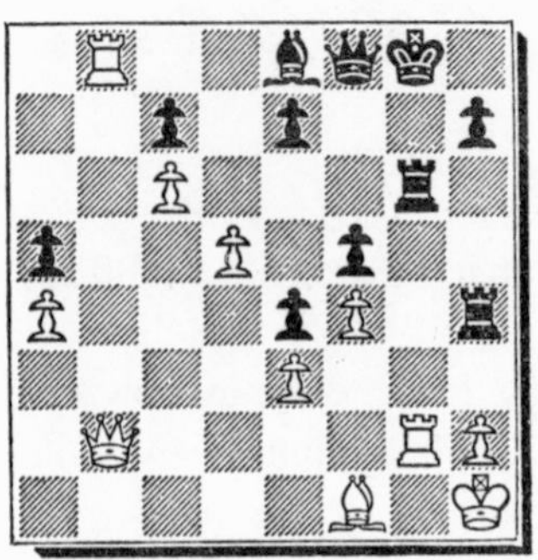

BLACK

DIAGRAM 79

WHITE *to play*

White's Rook on the King Knight file pins the Black Rook on the same file (an absolute pin). In addition, the White Rook on Queen Knight 8 pins the Black Bishop (a relative pin, as in this case Black's Queen is the screened piece).

So White operates with two pins. But in order to win in the quickest way, White must bring in still another theme – the queening power of the Pawn. This guides us to an astonishing, forcing, violent thrust:

1 **P–Q6**!! ....

As Black's Rook on King Knight 3 is pinned, he cannot play .... RxQP.

Meanwhile White threatens *2* PxBP, followed by *3* P–B8/Q. He also threatens *2* P–Q7 followed by *3* RxB or *3* PxB/Q.

And for good measure, White threatens *2* B–B4 ch, with consequences that we shall soon examine.

1 .... **KPxP**

This is about the only other move that Black has left – although White demolishes it at once.

2 **B–B4** ch ....

This forcing, violent check leaves Black without recourse, for if *2* .... Q–B2; *3* RxB mate!

2	**B–B2**

Black should resign.

3 **RxR** ch	**PxR**
4 **RxQ** ch	**KxR**
5 **Q–B6**	**Resigns**

Black's situation is hopeless.

The Knight fork

This tactical trick shares honors with the pin as being among the most frequently used devices that are both forcing and violent.

The Knight fork is a *double attack.* It is peremptory in effect and embarrassing to parry. Often a Knight fork is a *check,* and in such cases it is even more powerful; for, when the hostile King moves away, the remaining attacked unit becomes the Knight's legitimate prey.

In Diagram 80, which is the setting for no less than three Knight forks, we can observe the relentless thrust of the Knight fork.

BLACK

DIAGRAM 80

WHITE *to play*

It requires a good eye for Knight-forking possibilities to hit on White's procedure here.

1 **NxBP!**	....

Surprise! This forcing, violent move *forks Black's Queen and Rook* and thus leaves Black no choice. (As you will see later on, White can also start the Knight-forking sequence with *1* N–K7 ch, but we choose *1* NxBP! because it has more surprise value.)

1	**BxN/B3**
2 **N–K7** ch	....

A second *Knight fork.* This forcing, violent check forks Black's King and Bishop. Obviously Black's King must move, thus granting White the irresistible Knight fork which he has had in mind.

2	**K** moves
3 **NxB**	....

Forking Black's Queen and Rook. Black must move his Queen, allowing the Rook to be captured. The result of White's forcing, violent Knight forks is that he wins the Exchange and a Pawn. With this material advantage he should be able to win fairly easily.

OF COURSE, Knight forks do not always exist freshly minted in every given position. Sometimes we must prepare the proper setting. At first this may seem difficult; indeed, if you know very little about Knight forks, it *is* difficult.

However, if you follow the basic idea of looking for forcing, violent moves – moves that are likely to be checks or captures, or both – your quest becomes much, much easier. Take Diagram 81 as a case in point.

BLACK

DIAGRAM 81

WHITE *to play*

Imagine that you have White in this position. At first sight it would seem that you are in a bad way. Your Rook is attacked, and so is your Knight. You are faced with a decisive loss of material, it seems.

However, if you are aware of the power of forcing, violent moves, you can save the game. In fact, you can win!

1 **RxP** ch! ....

And this move, which on the face of it seems fantastic, is the right way, despite the fact that it seems to throw away a whole Rook for nothing.

Note that this is a forcing, violent move, a check and a capture. It is more – a *double attack* on Black's King and Queen which forces Black's hand by setting the stage for a winning Knight fork.

1 .... **QxR**

Black has no choice!

2 **N–K7** ch ....

This second forcing, violent move is just what the doctor ordered – a *Knight forking check* that simultaneously attacks King and Queen.

2 .... **K–B2**

Again Black has no choice. He *must* get out of check, leaving his Queen in the lurch.

3 **NxQ**	**KxN**

With Queen and two Pawns against Rook and Knight (see page 20) White will win without any trouble. The game might plausibly continue:

4 **Q–R4**	....

Attacking Black's Rook Pawn.

4	**P–R4**
5 **Q–N3**	....

Attacking Black's Knight Pawn.

5	**P–N4**
6 **Q–B3**	....

Again attacking Black's Rook Pawn.

6	**P–R5**
7 **P–K5** dis ch	....

Attacking Black's King Bishop Pawn, which cannot be saved because Black *is in check*. White's maneuvers with the Queen are a wonderful example of the tremendous power of this piece.

7	**K–N3**
8 **PxP**	....

Now White is three Pawns ahead, and his passed King Bishop Pawn is only two squares away from the queening square. White wins easily.

IN DIAGRAM 82, too, we are confronted with the problem of creating a setting for a devastating Knight fork. We have a valuable hint in the fact that the Black Queen is unprotected. (If you recall, this was the decisive factor in the play that evolved from Diagram 78.)

To create the appropriate setting for a Knight fork, we need a forcing, violent move. (Note how, time after time, this tried-and-true formula proves spectacularly successful.)

1 **QxP** ch!!	....

Superb play! A player working without the aid of our special formula would be highly unlikely to find this magnificent move. But, aided by the formula, he is able to find the most brilliant moves.

In this case, we have an astonishing Queen sacrifice, a forcing and violent check and capture. Black has no choice.

1	**KxQ**
2 **N–N5** ch	....

The point. This Knight forking check is forcing and violent. And, remember once more, it works because Black's Queen is *unguarded.*

2	**K–N1**
3 **NxQ**	....

And now the second point. Here we have a triple (!) Knight fork: the Knight attacks both Rooks and the Bishop. Black must save his Bishop, after which White plays NxR and then RxP, with two Pawns and the Exchange ahead. This gives him an easy win.

AS WE HAVE SEEN from earlier examples, the search for forcing, violent moves often guides us to the discovery of improbable-looking moves that most players would never dream of. Sometimes these possibilities are exceptionally well hidden. This is the case in Diagram 83, where many players would unsuspectingly pass over an opportunity for two exquisite Knight forks.

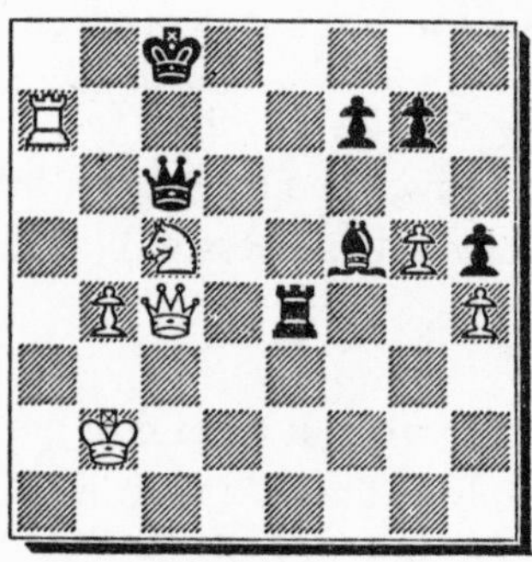

BLACK

DIAGRAM 83

WHITE *to play*

White's Queen is attacked by the hostile Rook. White's Knight is pinned, as *1* NxR would be answered by *1* .... QxQ. Most players, observing this, would retreat the White Queen to a safe spot.

But as we look into the position more deeply, we see an opportunity for a Knight fork! So White temporarily sacrifices his Queen:

1 **NxR!** ....

Because this is a violent move – a capture – it enables White to foresee his opponent's forced reply, after which a Knight-forking check looms up.

1 .... **QxQ**
2 **N–Q6 ch** ....

Another forcing, violent move. Black has only one reply.

2 .... **K–N1**

But Black has a *threat!* On 3 NxQ (what else?) he will reply 3 .... KxR, when the material will be even, and White's exertions will have turned out to be futile.

Shall we conclude, then, that White has simply wasted time – or is there some way to remedy the situation? Yes, there is; White creates the setting for a *second* Knight-forking check by now interpolating a forcing, violent move.

3 **R–N7** ch!!	....

This forcing, violent move is a check. In a moment we shall see why White wants to force Black to capture the Rook on his Queen Knight 2 square instead of on his Queen Rook 2 square.

3	**K–R1**
4 **NxQ**	**KxR**

Now everything becomes clear: *Black has been maneuvered into position for a second Knight forking check!*

5 **N–Q6** ch	**K** moves
6 **NxB**	....

Beautiful play by White. With a Knight ahead he has an easy win, as his Knight massacres the Black Pawns.

THUS we see repeatedly that it is one of the signs of a good player to create settings for *Knight forks.* The more compelling the consequences of that fork, the more peremptory is the need for creating such settings. The master sees these settings instinctively, because his mind is attuned to the devastating possibilities involved in the Knight fork. Diagram 84 offers a fine example.

White can play *1* NxB ch – a forcing move, because it is a check. But Black simply replies *1* .... QxN, and nothing is gained. So a good player would ask himself, "Can the Black Queen be enticed away from the protection of the Bishop?"

This is the kind of question that practically answers itself.

The question leads the player into a search for some forcing, violent move that will menace the Queen and force her to renounce her protection of the Bishop.

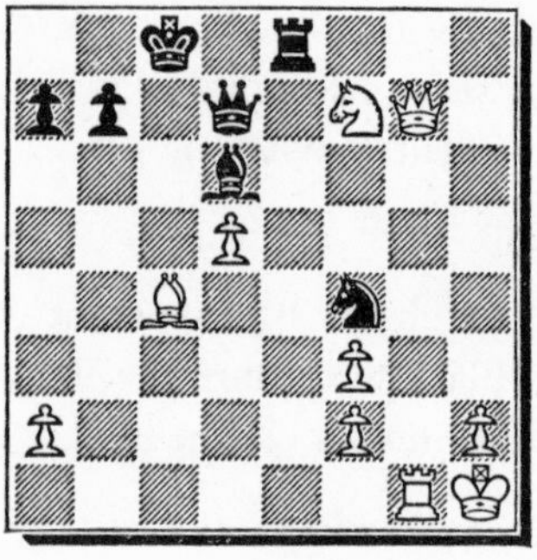

BLACK

DIAGRAM 84

WHITE *to play*

1 B–N5! ....

It goes against good judgment to move a piece where it has no protection. But White knows what he is about. He attacks the Black Queen, which cannot capture the boisterous Bishop because of the ferocious reply *2* NxB ch – a forcing, violent *Knight forking check* which would win the Queen.

1 .... Q–K2
2 BxR ....

Another forcing, violent move – this time a capture. Black cannot retake, for if *2* .... QxB, we again have the setting for a murderous Knight-forking check: *3* NxB ch winning the Queen.

So White remains a Rook ahead – an overwhelming superiority in material.

VERY OFTEN the common winning tactical tricks involve the application of more than one theme. Such harmonious combinations produce a very pleasing effect. This is charmingly illustrated in Diagram 85.

The feature that stands out here is that Black's Queen is stationed in front of his King on the long diagonal. The question is, how can White turn this to his advantage by creating a pin? The answer, as usual, is that he must find some forcing, violent moves. To wit:

1 **RxB!** ....

This forcing, violent move – a capture – initiates action on the long diagonal.

1 .... **PxR**

Naturally Black must recapture, as he cannot remain a Rook down.

But now we ask ourselves: what does White have to show for his sacrifice of the Exchange? To convince us, he must produce another forcing, violent move.

2 **BxP!** ....

Pinning the Black Queen, which screens the Black King from attack. This forces Black's reply.

2 .... **QxB**

The consequence of White's forcing, violent move. But now the setting for a decisive *Knight-forking check* has been created.

3 **NxBP** ch ....

This forcing, violent Knight-forking check wins Black's Queen because his King Knight Pawn is pinned by White's Queen.

So far in this chapter we have acquired two important tactical weapons: the pin and the Knight fork. There are several others with which we need to familiarize ourselves.

Double attacks

When a single unit simultaneously attacks two hostile units, we have one of the most economical, forcing, and violent moves that are available in the whole range of chess play.

The Knight fork is perhaps the most familiar of all double attacks. But all the other chessmen have this power of double attack, and the possibilities and varieties that may arise in an actual game are virtually limitless. Here we can give only a few to illustrate the point.

In Diagram 86 we see how the vast powers of the Queen can be unleashed for a double attack which aims in two divergent directions.

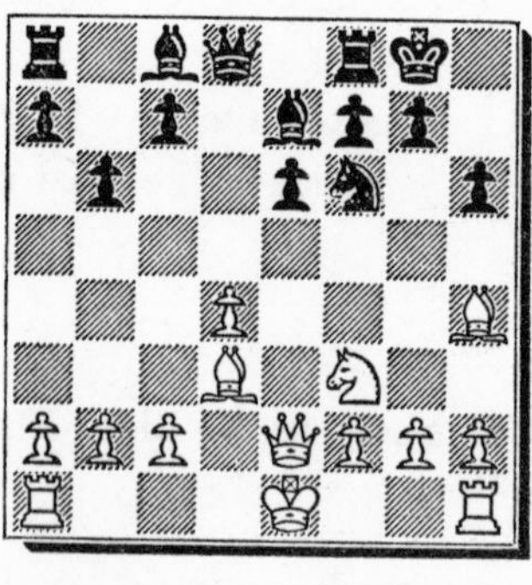

BLACK

DIAGRAM 86

WHITE *to play*

In this case, the key to White's double attack lies in the fact that Black's Queen Rook is momentarily unprotected. White must strike at once, and to do this he needs forcing, violent moves. The first of these is a capture:

1 BxN !	BxB
2 Q–K4	....

Now we see the reason for White's previous move. He needed to create a mate threat at King Rook 7, and he had to make it possible to bring his Queen to King 4. And now, after 2 Q–K4, he has the double threat of 3 Q–R7 mate in one direction, and the threat of 3 QxR in the other direction.

Black cannot parry both threats. He must stop the mate by 2 .... P–N3, and thus loses his Rook.

IN DIAGRAM 87, too, it is *the search for the unprotected piece* that leads us to the right winning method. Most players would notice that Black's Rook at King 7 is attacking a White Knight. To save the piece, they would very likely play *1* R–B2 or *1* QR–Q1. Such a defensive move is good enough as far as it goes. But we want to play forcing, violent moves; and from that point of view, defensive moves will not serve.

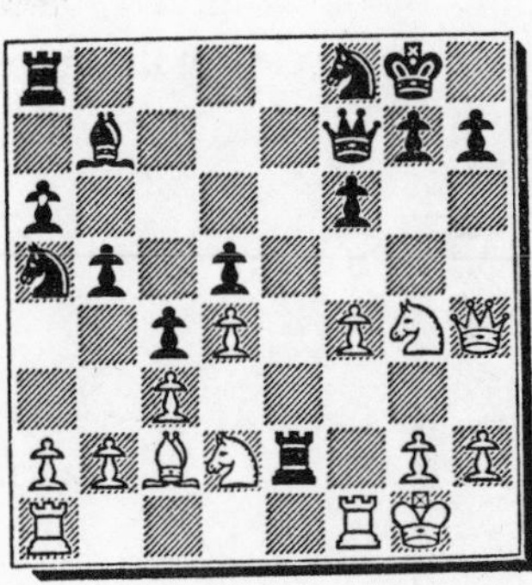

BLACK

DIAGRAM 87

WHITE *to play*

When we study the situation in Diagram 87 more closely, we realize that Black's Rook on King 7 is *unprotected.* (In previous situations we realized that this insight is often the key to winning play.)

Once White realizes this, he is inspired to look for forcing, violent moves. Therefore:

1 **N–R6** ch! ....

A *Knight-forking check* that attacks Black's King and Queen. Obviously Black must capture.

1 .... **PxN**

Now White is ready to take advantage of the unprotected state of Black's Rook at King 7.

2 **Q–N4** ch ....

Double attack: White gives check and also attacks Black's exposed Rook. Black is helpless against this forcing, violent move.

2 .... **K–R1**
3 **QxR** ....

By means of the double attack White has won the Exchange and should win in due course.

IN OUR ATTEMPTS to find the ideal forcing, violent forcing move, timing is always vital. This is clearly illustrated in the play that follows from Diagram 88.

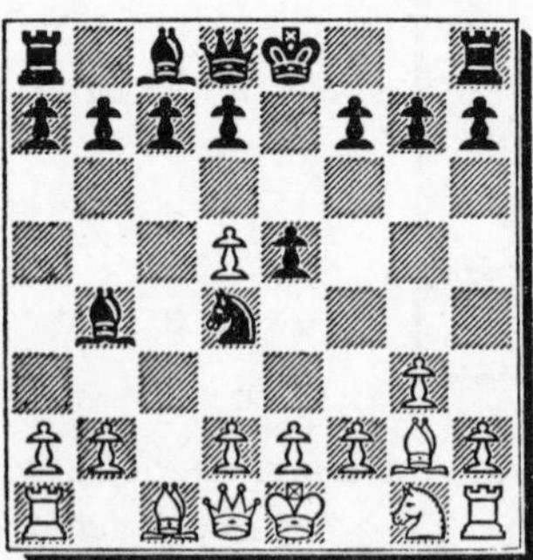

BLACK

DIAGRAM 88

WHITE *to play*

The immediate attack by *1* Q–R4 means nothing, as Black can defend in a variety of ways, for example *1* .... Q–K2 or *1* .... B–B4.

But, by selecting the right forcing, violent move, White can set up a winning *double attack.*

1 P–K3! ....

This leaves Black helpless. His Knight is attacked and must retreat. But there is no good retreat. If *1* .... N–N4 White plays *2* Q–R4 with a double attack that wins one of Black's menaced pieces. And if *1* .... N–B4, White plays *2* Q–N4, again with a double attack that wins one of Black's menaced pieces.

IN DIAGRAM 89 we see one of the most beautiful examples of double attack ever conceived on the chessboard.

White is a Pawn ahead and in the ordinary course of events he should win after a long, grueling endgame. Instead, seeking a forcing, violent move, he finds an amazing continuation.

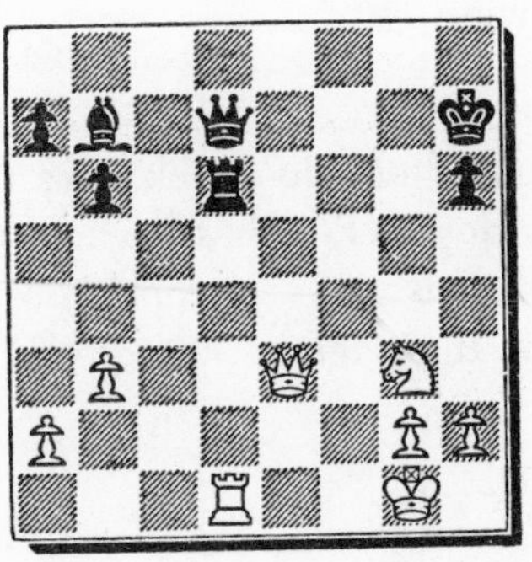

BLACK

DIAGRAM 89

WHITE *to play*

White's first move is so surprising that it looks like a blunder.

1 QxP ch!! ....

Certainly a forcing, violent move, as Black must capture the Queen. But is this Queen sacrifice sound? Black has two ways of capturing. Obviously *1* .... RxQ will not do, for then White has the *double attack* *2* RxQ ch, which wins Black's Bishop.

Shrinking from this forcing, violent move, Black tries a different way:

1	KxQ

And now it would seem that White has shot his bolt. However:

2 RxR ch	....

Another forcing, violent move – a double attack and capture with check.

2	QxR

Now it turns out that White's double attacks have created the perfect setting for a *Knight-forking check:*

3 N–B5 ch	K moves
4 NxQ	....

When we take stock of the situation, we find that all of White's exertions have achieved nothing more than the win of a "measly little Pawn!" However, with two Pawns ahead, White has a fairly easy endgame win.

SO FAR our examples of double attack have displayed the prowess of the Queen. However, as has been pointed out, the other pieces – and the Pawns too – are capable of carrying out efficient double attacks. In Diagram 90 we see how it is done.

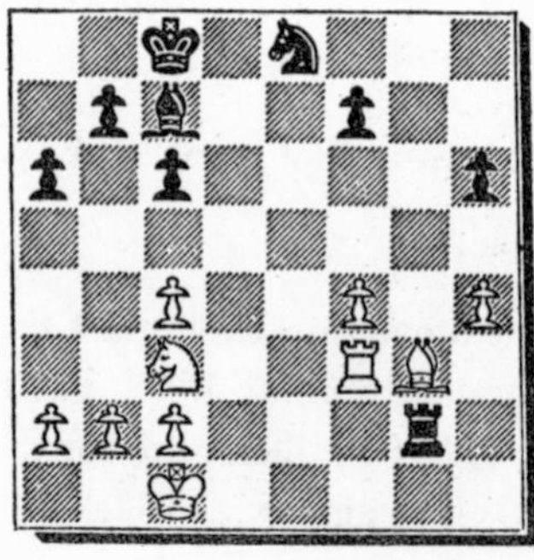

BLACK *to play*

DIAGRAM 90

WHITE

Black is definitely the aggressor here. His Rook, powerfully posted on the seventh rank, keeps the White Bishop under attack. His Bishop has a fine diagonal and attacks White's King Bishop Pawn, which is weak because it cannot be defended by a Pawn and must be defended by a piece.

White's pieces, on the other hand, have little scope. His Rook has the menial tasks of defending the Bishop and the King Bishop Pawn. His Bishop is hemmed in by its own Pawns, and has to share the task of protecting the King Bishop Pawn.

How is Black to translate his undeniable advantages into tangible material gain? Once more we need a forcing, violent move:

1 . . . . **RxB**!

The Rook is sacrificed in order to set up a *double attack.*

2 **RxR** **BxP** ch

This forcing, violent move – a double attack *with check,* wins White's Rook. Thus Black comes out a piece ahead, with an easy win.

EVEN the "lowly Pawn" can do a powerful job of double attacking, we may see from Diagram 91.

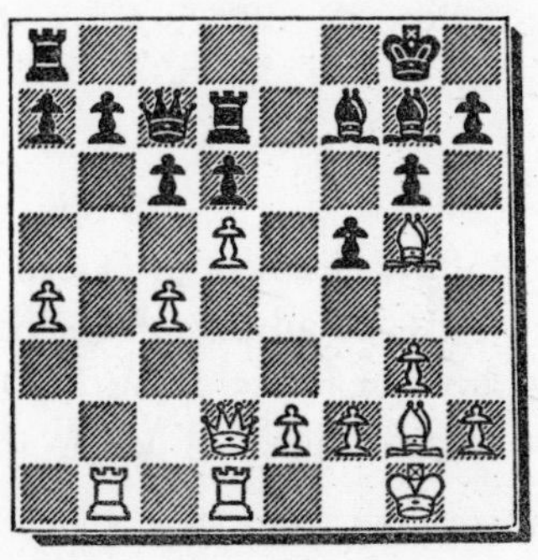

BLACK

DIAGRAM 91

WHITE *to play*

Examining this position, one has the instinctive feeling that the action of White's King Bishop on the long diagonal, the presence of the White Pawn on Queen 5, and the action of his Rook on the Queen Knight file all add up to some cogent possibilities.

But just how can White bring this hazy evaluation to life? How can he combine all these factors into a harmonious, decisive onslaught? Once again, what is needed is a forcing, violent move:

1 **RxP!** ....

Only a player seeking a forcing, violent move would hit on this Rook sacrifice.

1 .... **QxR**

Black has little choice.

2 **PxP** ....

Now everything becomes clear: by this double attack with the foremost Queen Bishop Pawn, White attacks Black's Queen and Rook.

2 .... **Q–B2**

Black must save his Queen.

3 **PxR** ....

And here is a *discovered attack:* in capturing the Rook, White opens up the long diagonal all the way for his King Bishop, uncovering an attack by that piece on Black's Rook at Queen Rook 1.

3 .... **R–N1**
4 **QxP!** ....

Now, regardless of whether Black exchanges Queens or not, White is prepared to queen his far-advanced Queen Pawn. Black will have to give up his remaining Rook for the new Queen. This will leave White with a whole Rook to the good. Black can just as well resign.

Discovered attack

This is a kind of double attack. A piece gets off a line to uncover ("discover") an attack by another piece standing on the same line.

The piece which moves out of the way does something which is forcing and violent – it may check, capture, or attack.

If the target of the second piece is a King, we have a "discovered check" (page 93). If both pieces give check, we have a "double check" (page 94).

If the target of the second piece is other than a King, we have a "discovered attack" – the subject of our present discussion.

The strength of the discovered attack is that it is always peremptory and often surprising – a combination of motifs that may utterly destroy the opponent's will or ability to resist. Almost invariably the discovered attack is aimed at an unprotected unit, and this too heightens its terrorizing powers!

In Diagram 92, for example, Black was rather slow on the uptake when it came to realizing the danger he was running into. The unprotected state of both Black Bishops is a direct invitation to trouble.

BLACK

DIAGRAM 92

WHITE *to play*

White's first move has an obvious point and a hidden point.

1 N–N5! ....

The *discovered attack*. By moving, the Knight opens up an attack by White's King Bishop on Black's Queen Bishop. Black cannot meet this forcing, violent move satisfactorily; for example:

1 .... **BxB**

This *seems* to save everything. But now we see the point of the discovered attack:

2 **BxN**! ....

Threatening *3* QxP mate! This, then, was the secondary purpose of the discovered attack *1* N–N5!

2 .... **P–N3**

Black's only defense to the mating threat.

3 **BxB** **BxR**
4 **BxR** ....

And no matter how Black plays, he remains a piece down.

Now return to Diagram 92, and let us try a different procedure for Black:

1 **N–N5**! **P–KR3**!?

Setting a trap for White. If now *2* BxB? (the obvious move), RxR; *3* RxR, PxN and Black has lost nothing.

Therefore White must choose a forcing, violent alternative.

2 **BxN**! ....

This makes all the difference. Remember, White is threatening checkmate!

2 .... **PxN**
3 **B/B6xB** ....

And again White has won a piece.

IN DIAGRAM 93 the winning procedure is also subtle, but perhaps easier to fathom than in the previous example.

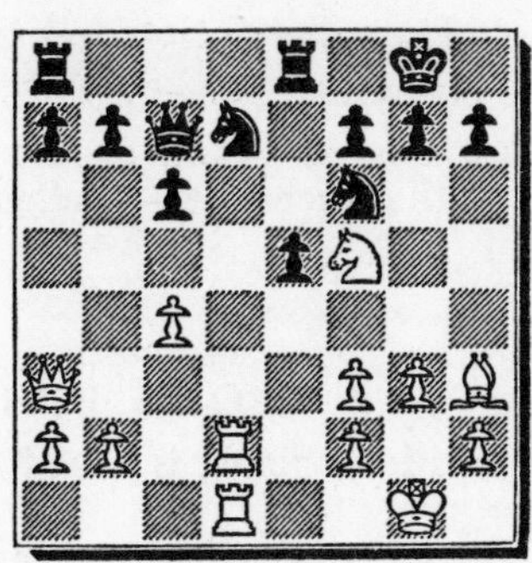

BLACK

DIAGRAM 93

WHITE *to play*

White attacks the Black Knight on Queen 7 through the action of his Rooks doubled on the Queen file. However, Black guards this Knight amply through defense by his other Knight and by his Queen.

Another aspect of the position claims our attention: White's Bishop bears down *indirectly* on Black's Knight on Queen 7. Somehow we sense instinctively that there must be some way for the Bishop to exploit the situation, especially since White's Knight can move off the diagonal *with check.*

There we have the elements we need: a twofold direct attack on the Black Knight; an additional attack – momentarily indirect – by White's Bishop; and a White Knight that can move out of the way by giving check.

Let us try a tentative sequence: *1* N–R6 ch, PxN; *2* BxN, NxB; *3* RxN, Q–N3, and while White has the better of it, the outcome is unclear.

And yet the winning idea is there. As in a jigsaw puzzle, its constituent elements must be rearranged. *What we need is a more forceful sequence.* And here it is:

1 **RxN!** ....

A forcing, violent capture. White sacrifices the Exchange – for a very good reason.

1 .... **NxR**

Black has no choice.

2 **RxN!** ....

And now a second sacrifice of the Exchange – another forcing, violent capture.

2 .... **QxR**

Black can save his Queen, say by 2 .... Q–N3. But in that case White, with two minor pieces for a Rook, is ahead in material (see page 20).

3 **N–R6** ch! ....

And here is the point of White's sacrificial play – a *discovered attack.* The Knight gives check and, in so doing, uncovers an attack on Black's Queen by the White Bishop. Black is given no time to save his Queen – a perfect example of a forcing, violent move.

3 .... **PxN**
4 **BxQ** ....

With his enormous material superiority – Queen and Bishop against two Rooks, White has an easy win.

IN DIAGRAM 94 the win depends on an even more delicate finesse, hinging on the fact that Black's Queen is *unprotected.*

BLACK

DIAGRAM 94

WHITE *to play*

White has three Pawns for the piece, which gives him approximate equality. What is more important, two of these Pawns are far advanced and passed. But where is the forcing, violent move which will assure White of winning?

Here is a priceless hint: if White plays *1* P–B7 dis ch, Black cannot reply *1* .... B–N2, for then comes *2* P–B8/Q ch, and Black's Bishop, being *pinned,* cannot capture the newly promoted Queen.

Such a forcing continuation generally offers promise of further success. So let us see how it works out:

1 **P–B7** dis ch **K–R2**

Forced, as we have seen.

2 **Q–B5** ch ....

Another forcing, violent move – another check.

2 .... **K–R1**

Again forced.

But how should White proceed now? If he tries *3* Q–K5 ch, Black simply moves his King again. Here is where finesse is required.

3 **Q–B6** ch!! ....

Once more we observe that Black dare not play *3* .... B–N2 because of *4* P–B8/Q ch.

3 .... **K–R2**

And now the stage is set for a brutal discovered attack:

4 **P–N6** ch! ....

The Pawn advances, giving check, *and at the same time "discovering" an attack by White's Queen on Black's unprotected Queen!* Thus White wins the Queen.

Other winning tactical tricks

The themes we have studied so far are the most commonly used and the ones that you will find most useful in practical play.

However, it is a good idea to conclude this chapter with a brief survey of several other tactical tricks which prove valuable on occasion.

The theme of "removing the guard" is illustrated in Diagram 95.

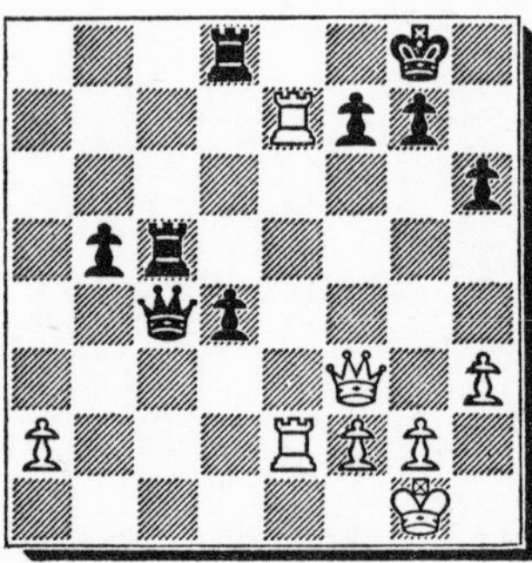

BLACK

DIAGRAM 95

WHITE *to play*

Black's Queen has the task of protecting his King Bishop Pawn. (Without this protection, White has a forced checkmate in two moves.)

White takes advantage of Black's predicament by playing a forcing, violent move:

1 **R–B2!** ....

For if *1* .... QxR; *2* QxP ch, K moves; *3* QxP mate.

1 .... **Q–Q4**
2 **RxR** ....

This forcing, violent move – a capture – makes life intolerable for Black. He cannot retake, for *2* .... QxR would allow the checkmate previously pointed out. Black must therefore resign.

IN DIAGRAM 96 we see a related theme, that of the "overworked piece." It is based on the fact that a piece which has more than one protective assignment is particularly vulnerable to attack. Black's Queen is again the target.

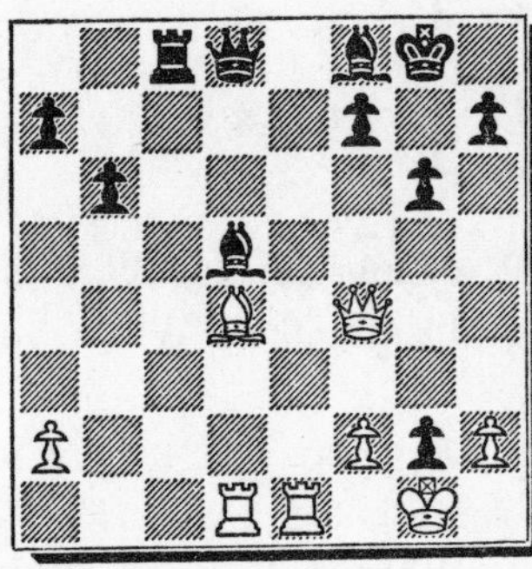

BLACK

DIAGRAM 96

WHITE *to play*

Black's Queen has a vital defensive task: to prevent White from playing Q–B6 followed by Q–R8 mate.

White craftily exploits the vulnerable position of Black's Queen by giving her a second defensive task:

1 **R–K8!** ....

This forcing, violent move leaves Black's Queen without one good move.

1 .... **QxR**
2 **Q–B6** ....

And Black is helpless against the coming Q–R8 mate.

COMBINATIONS to take advantage of the opponent's unguarded first rank should also be included among the forcing, violent moves.

This theme appears to good advantage in Diagram 97.

BLACK *to play*

DIAGRAM 97

WHITE

With the advantage of the Exchange ahead, Black is bound to win in the long run. However, his pin along White's first rank enables him to win rapidly.

While you will find the following play delightfully brilliant, bear in mind that basically it represents the *superior power of the Rook against the Knight*. Without this superior power, Black's brilliant play would be impossible.

1 .... **Q–Q5** ch!

A forcing, violent move. White cannot reply *2* Q–K3 ???, as this would lose his Queen, thanks to the *pin* on the Knight.

And in reply to *2* Q–B2 Black can play *2* .... QxP or *2* .... QxQ ch; *3* KxQ, R–N7 ch; *4* K–B3, RxRP, increasing his material advantage.

2 **K–R1** ....

Now White's King no longer guards the Knight. This protective task therefore devolves exclusively on White's Queen.

2 .... **QxP !**

A forcing, violent capture, coupled with attack on White's Queen.

White must not play *3* QxQ ??? allowing *3* .... RxN mate! This illustrates the power of the Rook on the *vulnerable first rank*. It might also be considered an example of "removing the guard" – the guard being White's Queen.

3 Q–Q3 Q–K5 !

Repeating his pseudo sacrifice in order to drive away the White Queen.

4 **Q–N5 ....**

Clearly, if *4* QxQ ???, RxN mate.

4 **.... Q–K8**

Threatening mate in two, and forcing White's reply.

5 K–N1 Q–K6 ch

This time definitively driving off the White King.

6 K–R1 Q–B7 !

Nicely played. He reinforces the *pin* in a way that makes it impossible for the White King to protect the Knight. White must resign.

WE HAVE NOW acquired a good insight into the forcing, violent moves that win games: checkmates, checks, captures, Pawn promotions, tactical tricks, and the like. In the remaining chapters we will see how these themes are applied in various facets of practical play.

POSITIONS FOR FURTHER STUDY

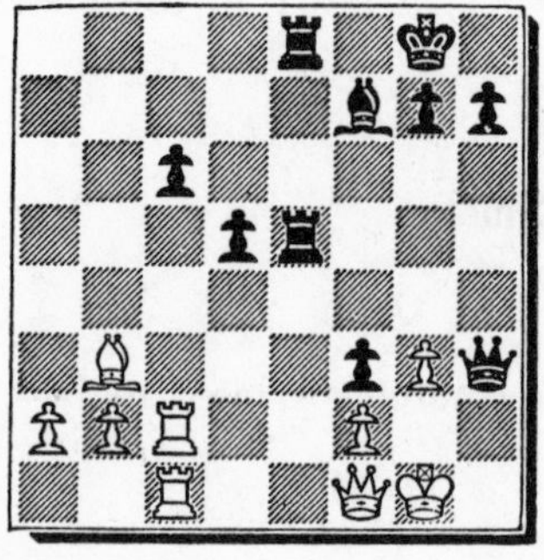

BLACK *to play*

DIAGRAM 98

WHITE

On the face of it, a disagreeable situation for Black. White offers the exchange of Queens, and whether Black exchanges or moves away his Queen, he loses his Queen Bishop Pawn. What is his best course?

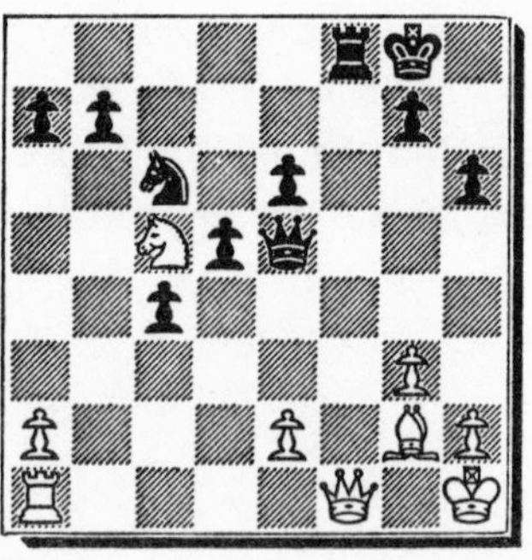

BLACK

DIAGRAM 99

WHITE *to play*

White is a piece ahead, but Black has three extra Pawns—roughly equivalent in value. Unless White can find an incisive continuation, he faces a long-drawn-out struggle.

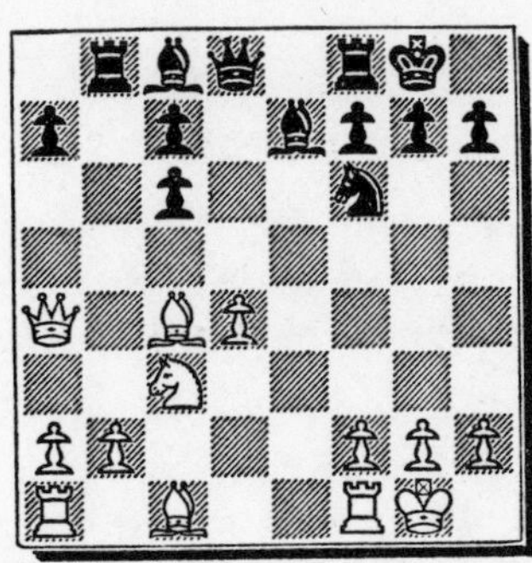
BLACK *to play*

DIAGRAM 100

WHITE

Black is faced with a disagreeable dilemma, as his Queen Rook Pawn and foremost Queen Bishop Pawn are attacked by the White Queen. Note, by the way, that Black dare not capture White's Queen Pawn (why?).

How should Black continue?

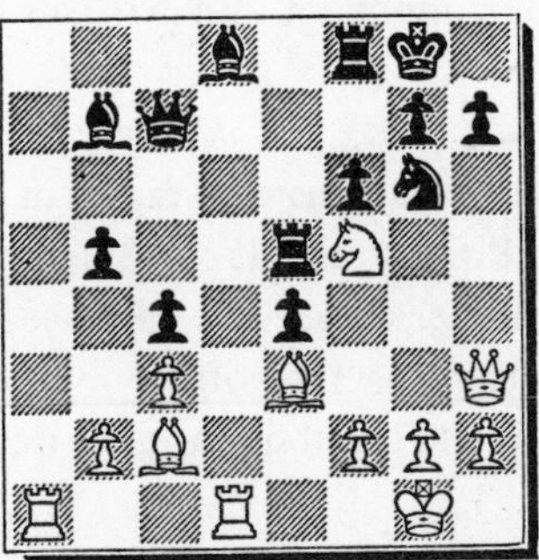
BLACK

DIAGRAM 101

WHITE *to play*

Black is a Pawn ahead with an apparently solid position. Yet White can turn the situation to his advantage. How?

6. *Threats*

Chess, like life, is full of unforeseen happenings and surprises. To know about forcing, violent moves and their power is not enough. For your opponent also has this resource at his disposal.

In its very essence, chess is a struggle – a struggle of ideas, of clashing wills, of possibilities that may or may not happen. Among such possibilities are threats and traps. Whether or not they come off as planned, whether or not they are seen by one player or both – these are problems that often determine the fate of a game. Threats and traps contribute a great deal to the color and drama of chess.

The nature of a threat

A threat is a form of attack. (We use the word "attack" here as a short-cut term for the various kinds of forcing, violent moves that we have discussed in this book.)

A threat, by its very nature, involves a possibility of winning by force. To see your opponent's threats – or rather, to *foresee* them, is absolutely essential if you are to become a good chess player. Failing to perceive the threat means that you are left helplessly exposed to the danger that hangs over you like the sword of Damocles.

To be sure, there are threats and threats. You may see through your opponent's threat and let him play it all the same; you may see farther ahead than he does, or more clearly, and you may be well aware that his threat lacks the power that he thinks it possesses.

On the other hand, your appraisal of the threat may be wide of the mark; it may turn out to be far more powerful than you imagined.

Other possibilities are even more nebulous. Your opponent may have a threat that he does not even see; still, if you perceive the threat you cannot risk the possibility of his being unaware of it.

All these uncertainties make chess more interesting; they also make it more difficult. But of this you may be assured – that if you concentrate on the forcing, violent moves, you will have no difficulty in seeing through your opponent's threats and devising your own threats.

Thus, in Diagram 102, White rightly depends on the fact that Black's Queen is badly out of play; indeed, there is a deplorable lack of cooperation among all his pieces.

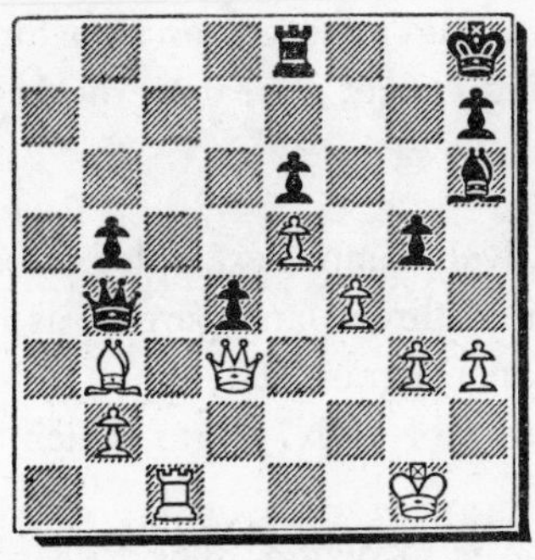

BLACK

DIAGRAM **102**

WHITE *to play*

White can of course play *1* B–B2 threatening *2* QxRP mate. But that would be all wrong, as Black would rid himself of the worst drawback in his position by playing *1* .... Q–K2. In that case, his Queen *would no longer be out of play,* and his pieces would be working together in good style.

This suggests a valuable moral: when you see a threat, do not snap at it. Make sure you are executing it in its most powerful, most convincing, most drastic form. That is what White does here – coming up with something much more decisive than the first puny version we have examined.

1 **R–B7!** ....

A forcing, violent move which threatens mate – and it has the added virtue of ruling out *1* .... Q–K2 as a defense.

If Black replies *1* .... B–N2 then 2 B–B2 leaves Black helpless, as he has no way to defend against the threat of 3 QxRP mate.

1 .... **R–K2**

Naïvely hoping for 2 RxR, QxR, after which the mating attack would be over.

2 **R–B8** ch! ....

Another forcing, violent move – a check.

2 .... **K–N2**
3 **B–B2** Resigns

Now the mating threat *4* QxRP mate comes in a form that leaves Black helpless; his King cannot retreat to the first rank.

THIS WAS a comparatively simple example; threats can involve much more complicated thrusts and parries, as may be seen in the play evolving from Diagram 103.

White has a potential threat of Q–N7 mate which is prevented by the Black Queen.

White's logical continuation is to play a Rook to King 1 – a forcing, violent move which attacks the protective Queen.

But a vital finesse is involved. Which Rook should White

BLACK

DIAGRAM **103**

WHITE *to play*

---

play to King 1? Believe it or not, one Rook move wins; the other Rook move loses!

Here is the right way:

1 **KR–K1 !** ....

This forcing, violent move creates intolerable problems for Black. In order to parry White's mating threat, he can only retreat *1* .... Q–B2; but then comes a second forcing, violent move: *2* R–K7 ! blocking off the Queen's protection against the mating threat.

Nor will *1* .... B–K5 do, for then White plays *2* RxB ! winning, as *2* .... QxR allows *3* Q–N7 mate, while *2* .... PxR allows *3* QxQ ch followed by mate!

But Black has one more try: *1* .... R–KN1. Then there follows *2* QxR ch!, RxQ; *3* RxQ, RxP ch; *4* K–B1 (not *4* K–R1 ??, R–N1 dis ch and *Black* forces checkmate with his vicious discovered check!), RxRP. Now Black attacks the Knight and also threatens .... R–R8 ch winning White's Rook at Queen Rook 1. However, White has a perfect parry with *5* RxKBP !! (protecting the Knight) and *5* .... R–R8 ch; *6* K–B2, RxR will not do because of *7* R–B8 mate. *Black is vulnerable on his first rank.*

This kaleidoscopic series of forcing, violent moves is thrilling though difficult to calculate. But now back to Diagram 103 and let us see what happens on *1* QR–K1 ??

1 QR–K1 ??	R–KN1 !

A winning *counterthreat* here!

2 QxR ch	RxQ
3 RxQ	RxP ch

Now White's King *must* go to Rook 1!

4 K–R1	R–N1 dis ch

And Black forces checkmate in two more moves.

The difference between *1* KR–K1 ! and *1* QR–K1 ??, then, is that the former move makes room for a later K–B1, which enables White to win; whereas the latter move condemns White to K–R1, which loses.

IN DIAGRAM 104, on the other hand, we again have a clean-cut threat which allows of no satisfactory defense.

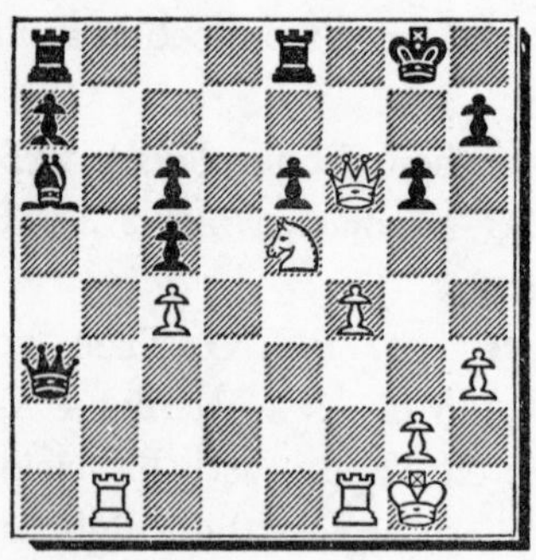

BLACK

DIAGRAM 104

WHITE *to play*

With Black's Queen hopelessly out of play, the combined action of White's Queen and Knight is bound to be devastating. White begins with a forcing, violent move:

1 N–N4	....

Threatens *2* N–R6 mate.

1	**P–R3**
2 QxNP ch	**....**

Another forcing, violent move – a check. If now *2* .... K–R1; *3* N–B6, R–K2; *4* Q–R6 ch, R–R2; *5* QxR mate.

2	**K–B1**
3 NxP	**....**

Another forcing, violent move – White threatens *3* Q–B7 mate.

3	**R–K2**

Defending the threat, but blocking the Black King's escape.

4 Q–N8 mate

IN DIAGRAM 105 there is no doubt that Black has a winning attack. The question is, how does he win in the quickest way?

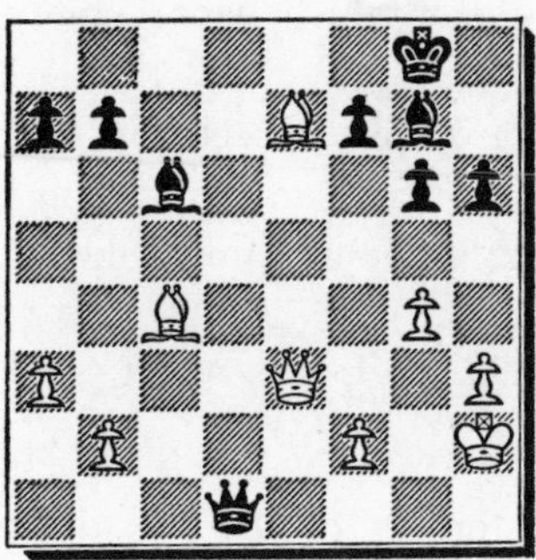

BLACK *to play*

DIAGRAM **105**

WHITE

Black's most obvious course is *1* .... Q–KR8 ch; *2* K–N3, Q–N7 ch; and while this ought to win, there is no immediate victory in sight.

Instead, Black carries out his attack in a manner which is much more subtle and much more conclusive.

1 .... **B–K4** ch!!

A forcing, violent move – a check.

If 2 QxB, then 2 .... Q–B6! (threatens .... Q–N7 mate); 3 Q–N3, Q–R8 mate.

2 **P–B4** ....

This seems to save the day for White.

2 .... **BxP** ch!!

A new, deadly surprise. This forcing, violent check attacks White's King and Queen, and therefore leaves White no choice.

3 **QxB** **Q–KR8** ch

Another forcing, violent check.

4 **K–N3** **Q–KN8** ch!

Still another forcing, violent check.

5 **K–R4** **Q–K8** ch!
6 **Q–N3** **P–KN4** ch!

The final forcing, violent check which wins White's Queen after 7 BxNP, PxB ch, etc.

This beautiful, forcible line of play effectively teaches the lesson that where there is more than one threat, you must be careful to choose the strongest and most profitable threat.

Combined threats

The most powerful threats of all are those which involve a sustained menace, or those which pursue more than one goal. Once we bring in the theme of *double attack*, or of attack on more than one front, our chances of success are that much greater.

In Diagram 106, for example, White's double attack immediately drives Black's forces into hopeless disarray. To be sure,

White's contemplated *Knight-forking check* is formidable enough to terrify the most case-hardened opponent.

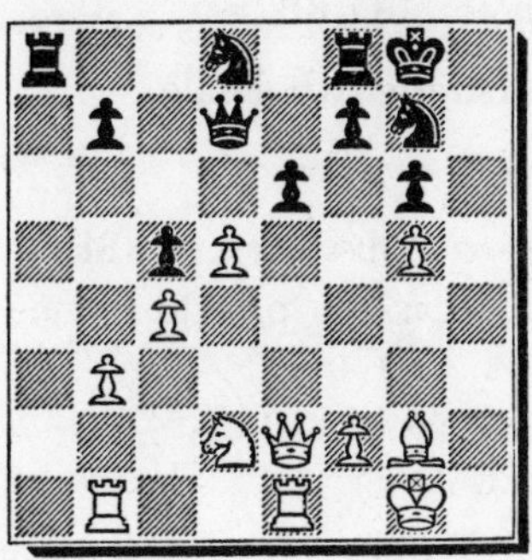

BLACK

DIAGRAM **106**

WHITE *to play*

White immediately spies out the weakness in the Black camp.

1 **N–K4!** ....

This forceful, violent move threatens N–B6 ch, forking Black's King and Queen. It also threatens NxP, winning a Pawn and giving White a very superior position.

In this sense it sets a sly trap, as it is tempting for Black to reply *1* .... Q–K2 ?? defending against both threats. In that event White replies *2* P–Q6 ! forcing *2* .... Q–K1 or *2* .... Q–Q2, whereupon *3* N–B6 ch wins Black's Queen after all.

1 .... **N–K1**

Black sees the trap and resigns himself to losing the Queen Bishop Pawn while he parries the main threat.

2 **NxP** **Q–K2**

Attacking the Knight, but White pays no attention.

3 **PxP!** ....

A forcing, violent capture. White sees that on *3* .... QxN he can play the Pawn fork *4* P–K7, attacking Black's King Rook and the Knight at Black's Queen 1. This would be disastrous for Black.

3 .... **R–R4**

Despair. After *3* .... PxP or *3* .... NxP, White wins at least another Pawn, with an easy win.

4 **PxP ch** **QxBP**

Any other move also loses material wholesale.

5 **B–Q5** ....

This forcing, violent move – a pin – wins the Black Queen. It did not take long for White's dashing play to reduce Black's position to rubble.

IN DIAGRAM 107 all of White's pieces are poised menacingly against Black's King side. Note particularly the White Rook on the open King Rook file; the White Queen, ready to take a hand on the open file; the White Bishop on Queen 4, with terrific sweep on the long diagonal.

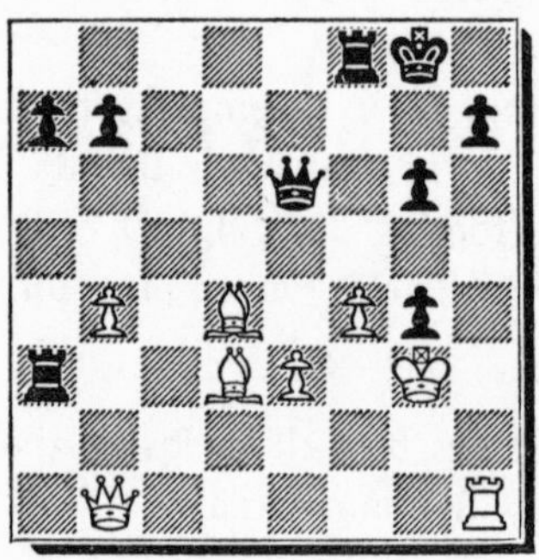

BLACK

DIAGRAM 107

WHITE *to play*

The most important element in White's threat mechanism is the combined action of his Rook on King Rook 1 and Bishop on Q4. This immediately results in a forcing, violent move:

1 **RxP!** ....

Threatening *2* R–N7 ch, K–R1; *3* Q–KR1 mate.

Black must take the obnoxious Rook, but then he runs into a mating attack.

1	KxR
2 Q–KR1 ch	....

Beginning a crushing series of forcing, violent checks.

2	K–N1
3 Q–R8 ch	K–B2
4 Q–N7 ch	K–K1
5 B–N5 ch	Resigns

Black has had enough, for if *5* .... K–Q1; *6* QxR ch, K–B2; *7* B–K5 ch and he must part with his Queen.

IN DIAGRAM 108 we meet a problem of great practical interest – the attack against a King which is exposed to attack. Black is in a bad way here, for not only is his King in the cross-fire of the enemy pieces; he lags badly in development and is thus in no position to give substantial aid to his seriously threatened King. White's pieces, on the other hand, are beautifully poised for action.

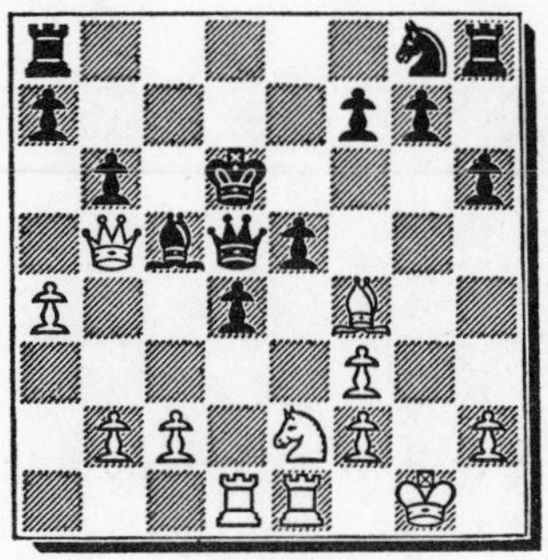

BLACK

DIAGRAM 108

WHITE *to play*

Thanks to the advantages already outlined, White is able to proceed in brilliant style:

1 NxP !!	....

Threatening *2* N–B5 ch above all, winning Black's Queen.

Note that Black cannot play *1* .... PxN, as his King Pawn is *pinned.*

1	**BxN**
2 **RxB** !	....

Another forcing, violent capture which leaves Black no choice.

2	**QxR**
3 **BxKP** ch	....

Another forcing, violent capture – a *double attack* which wins Black's Queen.

3	**QxB**
4 **QxQ** ch	Resigns

For after *4* .... K–Q2; *5* Q–Q5 ch or *4* .... K–B3; *5* Q–K4 ch, White's forcing, violent check wins Black's Queen Rook. A convincing example of the demolition of an exposed King's position.

IN DIAGRAM 109 we see how a latent threat can be transformed into a dynamic threat that brings quick victory.

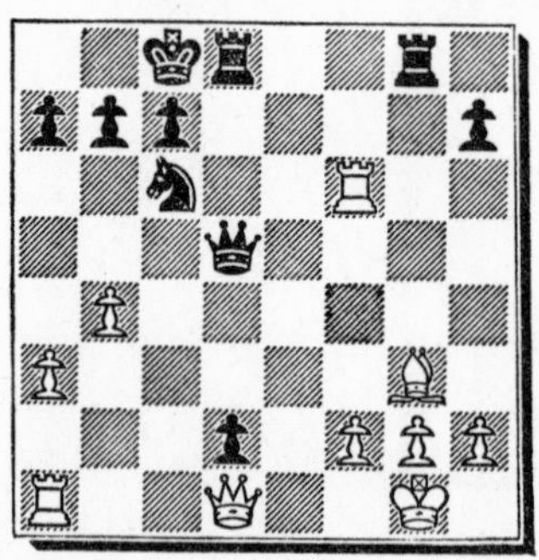

BLACK *to play*

DIAGRAM 109

WHITE

Black's far-advanced passed Queen Pawn is a standing menace to White, who must keep his Queen at Queen 1 to blockade the further advance of this powerful Pawn.

There are many ways for Black to win; one of them is

1 .... KR–K1 (threatening .... R–K8 ch, winning White's Queen). If then 2 P–B3 or P–B4, Black replies 2 .... Q–Q5 ch (*double attack!*) winning White's Rook at King Bishop 6.

However, Black chooses a different sequence which leads to most remarkable play.

1 .... **Q–Q5** !

This forcing, violent move is really a *double attack*. It threatens not only 2 .... QxR/B3, but also 2 .... QxR/R8 !; *3* QxQ, P–Q8/Q ch and mate next move.

White finds an ingenious though inadequate defense.

2 **R–B7** **QxR** !

With this forcing, violent capture Black sacrifices his Queen and proclaims that he is not afraid of White's coming *discovered check*.

3 **RxBP** ch **K–N1**
4 **R–Q7** dis ch **RxB** !

Black can also win with *4* .... K–R1, but the method he chooses is very pretty.

5 **RxR** ch **NxR**
6 **QxQ** **R–QB6** !

After this lovely move White resigns.

For if 7 QxR, P–Q8/Q ch (promotion to a Rook also wins) forces mate on the following move.

If White does not capture the Rook, Black plays 8 .... R–B8 ch, ensuring the disappearance of the White Queen and the promotion of his own Pawn. Black either forces checkmate on White's vulnerable first rank or else winds up with an overwhelming superiority in material. This is a splendid example of the enormous power of Pawn promotion.

AND IN DIAGRAM 110 we see still another facet of the Pawn's powers – the *Pawn fork*.

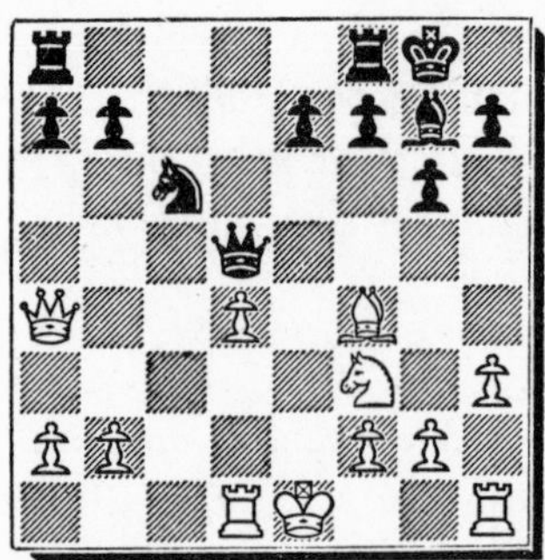

BLACK *to play*

DIAGRAM **110**

WHITE

Black attacks White's Queen Pawn three times, and White defends it three times. We might therefore expect Black to strengthen his threat against the Queen Pawn by playing *1* .... KR–Q1. This move would of course be quite good, but, thanks to the fact that White is not yet castled, Black can proceed against the Queen Pawn without any preliminaries.

1 .... **NxP** !!

A forcing, violent capture. Black is not afraid of 2 RxN, BxR; 3 QxB, QxQ; *4* NxQ, for then comes *4* .... P–K4 ! (Pawn fork – *double attack*); *5* BxP, R–K1 (now a *pin*); *6* P–B4, P–B3; *7* N–B3, PxB and Black has won the Exchange in return for a Pawn.

2 **NxN** **QxNP**

If now 3 R–KB1, the *double attack* 3 .... P–K4 wins easily.

3 **R–R2** **Q–K5** ch

Another forcing, violent check. Note that White cannot interpose *4* N–K2 ?? as this would lose his Queen. (In other words, his Knight is *pinned*.)

4 **B–K3** ....

He has nothing better. But this allows a forcing, violent threat to which there is no reply.

4 .... **B–K4** !

White resigns, as his attacked Rook is trapped!

IN DIAGRAM 111, too, superior development is the key to success. Black has castled, it is true, but he is so far behind in development that White's pieces have a field day. White's chief menace comes from his magnificently *centralized* Bishop at King 5 and his exclusive command of the King Bishop file. This combined pressure makes possible a whole series of mating threats and other forcing, violent moves.

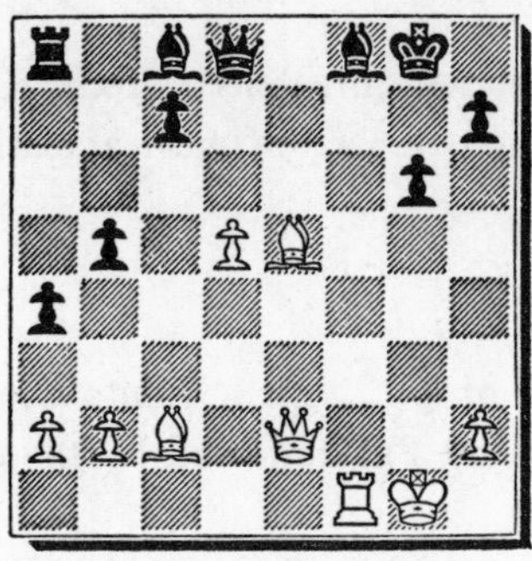

BLACK

DIAGRAM 111

WHITE *to play*

White starts with a mating threat:

1 **Q–B3** ....

This threatens 2 Q–B7 mate.

If *1* .... Q–K1 in reply; 2 Q–B6 threatens mate, leaving Black helpless.

And if *1* .... Q–K2; 2 P–Q6! (*discovered attack*) menaces Black's Queen and his Rook as well.

1 .... **B–B4** ch
2 **K–R1** ....

Note that .... Q–K1 and .... Q–K2 are still ruled out for the reasons given above.

2 .... **Q–B1**
3 **Q–N2** ....

Naturally White evades the exchange of Queens; but attacks

Black's Queen while he still retains control of the King Bishop file, and reserves threats of P–Q6 or BxNP. (The latter threat explains Black's reply.)

3	**Q–K1**
4 **P–Q6**	....

Another forcing, violent move which threatens 5 QxR and also 5 Q–Q5 ch.

4	**B–K3**
5 **R–B6**	....

And this forcing, violent move threatens 6 RxB, QxR; 7 QxR ch – and also 6 BxNP, PxB; 7 RxP ch with a mating attack.

5	**B–B2**
6 **RxB!**	....

Beautiful play! In the event of 6 .... QxR, White wins by 7 QxR ch, Q–B1; 8 QxQ ch, KxQ; 9 PxP followed by the queening of his Bishop Pawn.

On the other hand, if 6 .... KxR; 7 Q–Q5 ch, Q–K3; 8 Q–B3 ch!! forcing Black's King to the first rank so that White gains time by capturing his Rook *with check*.

6	**QxB**
7 **BxNP!**	Resigns

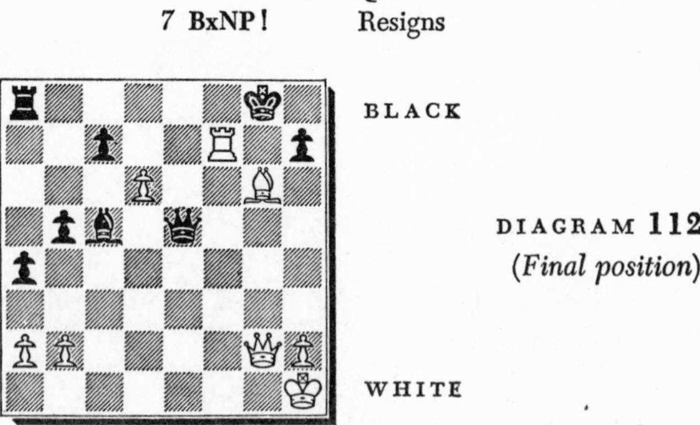

DIAGRAM **112**
(*Final position*)

White's threats are too much for his opponent.

Thus, if *7* .... PxB; *8* QxP ch and White mates next move.

If *7* .... Q–K8 ch; *8* R–B1, and in view of the threat of *9* QxR ch Black has nothing better than *8* .... QxR ch; *9* QxQ, PxB. But then comes *10* Q–N2 or Q–B3 and Black is helpless against the double threat of *11* QxR ch or *11* Q–Q5 ch winning the Bishop.

Most interesting are the consequences of Black's attempts to save his Rook. For example, if *7* .... R–K1; *8* BxP dbl ch!, K–R1 (not *8* .... KxR; *9* Q–N6 ch, K–B1; *10* Q–N8 mate); *9* R–K7! (illustrating the themes of *double attack* and *overworked piece*), and Black is lost, for if *9* .... RxR; *10* Q–N8 mate.

Or if *7* .... R–Q1; *8* BxP dbl ch!, K–R1; *9* B–K4! threatening R–R7 mate and also Q–R3 ch followed by mate.

This is a wonderfully instructive example of irresistible threats which make possible one forcing, violent move after another.

FOR OUR FINAL example of a winning threat we choose a position in which it takes ten moves to make the threat work. (See Diagram 113.) This sounds laborious, but it really isn't, because chess becomes very easy, once we have a basic idea that guides our thoughts in specific directions, and consequently eases the problem of selecting a move.

BLACK

DIAGRAM 113

WHITE *to play*

White's Queen and his Bishop on Queen Bishop 2 are actively involved in the attack, and his King Rook is about to take a hand in it too.

Black's pieces, on the other hand, have little scope and are awkwardly placed for defense. Worst of all, Black has created a target for attack by advancing his King Knight Pawn.

1 **P–B5!** ....

This threatens *2* P–B6, when Black will have to give up his Knight to stop *3* Q–N7 mate.

As *1* .... PxP would open up Black's castled position to a vicious attack, Black must find some other way to meet White's threat.

1 .... **Q–Q3**

Preventing *2* P–B6 and also preparing the possibility of .... Q–B1 in case of need.

2 **R–R1** ....

Threatening *3* B–R3, Q–B2; *4* P–B6 when Black again must give up his Knight because of the threatened *5* Q–N7 mate.

2 .... **Q–B1**
3 **Q–R4** ....

Retreating, but only temporarily, for now he has the terrible threat of *4* B–R3, Q–N2; *5* P–B6, Q–R1 and Black's Queen is buried forever.

3 .... **Q–K2**
4 **P–B6** **Q–K3**

Black is just barely managing to hold on. On *5* Q–R6 he can play *5* .... NxP.

5 **R–B3** ....

In order to play B–R3 without allowing .... QxKP ch in reply.

5 .... **PxP**

Black wins a Pawn, but the game will be decided on the other wing.

6	B–R3	QR–N1
7	QR–KB1	....

White has renewed his old threat. With his advanced King Bishop Pawn doubly defended, he threatens 8 Q–R6, forcing Black to lose a piece by .... NxP in order to stop Q–N7 mate.

BLACK *to play*

DIAGRAM 114

WHITE

Black finds the only defensive pattern that will enable him to hold on – for a little while.

7	....	K–R1

In order to play .... R–KN1 to guard against Q–N7 mate after White plays Q–R6.

8	R–K1	....

For reasons that will soon become clear, White plans to play R–B4. He therefore gives his King Pawn more protection.

8	....	R–N6

Black offers the sacrifice of the Exchange in order to obtain a passed Pawn that might divert White's attention from the King-side.

9	B–K7!	....

White disdains winning the Exchange, as he is intent on his

mating attack. With one of his Rooks gone from the King Bishop file, he needs more protection for his King Bishop Pawn when he plays Q–R6.

9	**RxP**
10 **Q–R6**	....

Threatening mate. White has made all his preparations.

10	**R–KN1**

Stopping the mate, but boxing in his King, which exposes him to a new mate threat.

11 **R–B4**!	Resigns

Black is helpless against White's last forcing move and the violent mate threat which it involves: *12* QxRP ch!, KxQ; *13* R–R4 mate. Thus, after much needed preparation, White finally executed his mate threat as originally planned from Diagram 113. (Note that if *11* .... P–N4; *12* QxRP mate.)

Counterthreats

From the threats we have studied so far, we might easily get the mistaken idea that threats always work. Some threats have a flaw; some turn out to be weaker than they seemed; some can be topped by a more powerful counterthreat. The demolition of a threat adds much to the dramatic and colorful qualities of chess.

In Diagram 115 we see a typical example of a threat which is easy to refute.

White, a piece down, threatens Q–KN7 mate. Black can defend himself with *1* .... Q–QB6, but he has a much more drastic method of meeting the threat:

1	**N–KB6** ch!

This forcing, violent check drives White into a checkmate position. If, for example, *2* K–R1, Black replies *2* .... N–N6 mate.

2 **PxN**	**Q–K7** ch

BLACK *to play*

DIAGRAM **115**

WHITE

---

3 **K–R1**	**QxBP** ch
4 **K** moves	**Q–B7** ch
5 **K–R1**	**N–N6** mate

By a series of forcing, violent checks Black has nullified White's checkmate threat by first enforcing checkmate himself.

IN DIAGRAM 116, White's threat to win a piece is put to shame by Black's counterthreat which involves a brusque checkmate menace.

BLACK *to play*

DIAGRAM **116**

WHITE

White is two Pawns ahead, and he attacks Black's Bishop. To defend the Bishop is easy enough, but Black would still be in a losing position because of his material minus.

What Black wants, therefore, is a counterthreat which will actually turn the tables, and give him a won game. Such a resource must necessarily be forcing and violent.

1 . . . . N–B5 !

Instead of bothering to protect his Bishop, Black attacks the White Queen and simultaneously threatens 2 . . . . Q–N7 mate.

2 PxN QxP

Again threatening checkmate. White has only one way out, but it isn't good enough: he must part with his Queen.

3 QxB QxQ

And Black wins easily with his material advantage. Black's counterthreat made mincemeat of White's original threat.

IN DIAGRAM 117 the player subjected to the threat does not have a mate counterthreat, but he nevertheless extricates himself neatly from what seems like a completely hopeless situation. In such situations, the search for counterplay requires even more aggressive spirit than it took to set up the original threat. Timorous players have been known to resign in the face of a threat that could have been parried by courageous and incisive measures.

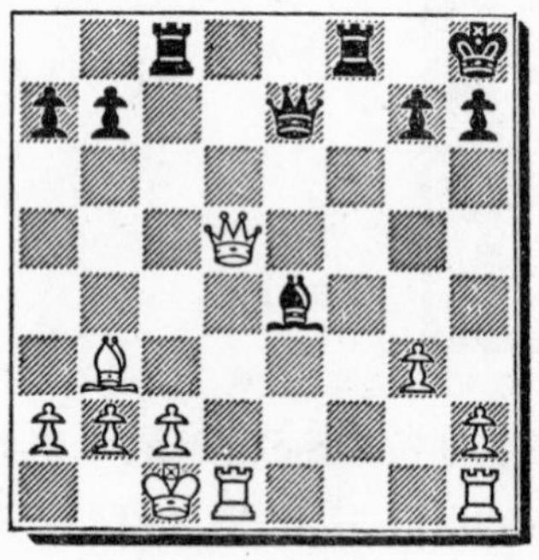

BLACK

DIAGRAM 117

WHITE *to play*

With a *double attack* on White's Queen and King Rook, Black seems to have a sure win. Yet White has no reason for despair: a forcing, violent move will stave off material loss.

1 **KR–K1!** ....

This *pin* works because Black's Queen is unprotected.

1 .... **BxQ**
2 **RxQ** ....

Now that the crisis is over, White's extra Pawn should win for him.

IN DIAGRAM 118 White, whose Queen is attacked, is well on the way to victory because of his material advantage (Bishop and Knight against Rook). He can do well enough by playing *1* Q–B7 threatening mate, for in that case he is bound to win Black's Queen Bishop Pawn (*1* .... R–Q2; *2* QxBP – or, much worse for Black, *1* .... Q–Q2 ??; *2* QxQ, RxQ; *3* R–N8 ch forcing mate on Black's *unprotected first rank*).

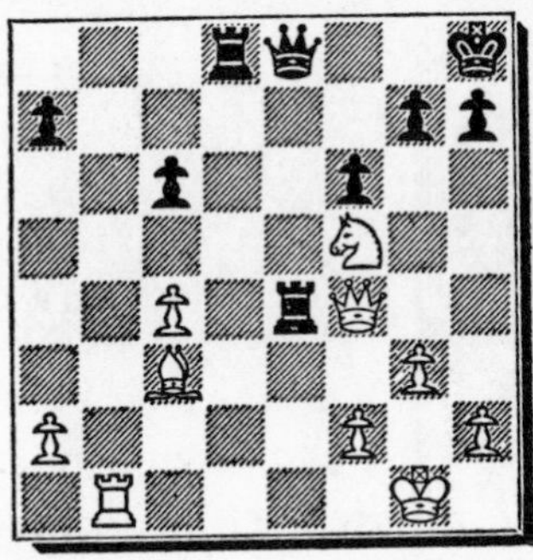

BLACK

DIAGRAM 118

WHITE *to play*

However, when subjected to a threat, we want to find the very best counterthreat, which in this case is:

1 **NxP!** ....

This forcing, violent capture involves a mating possibility: *1* .... KxN ??; *2* QxP ch, K–N1; *3* Q–N7 mate.

And since White, in addition to menacing Black's Queen, also threatens *2* QxP, Black has no choice.

1	**RxQ**
2 **NxQ**	....

Now the full power of White's counterthreat can be appreciated. No matter how Black plays, he must lose the Exchange, remaining a piece down.

For example: *2* .... RxN; *3* PxR – or *2* .... R–B4; *3* BxP ch, RxB; *4* NxR, etc. Of course, being ahead in material makes it easier to set effective counterthreats.

A STARTLING turnabout takes place in Diagram 119, for White *pins* and threatens to win Black's Queen and there seems to be nothing that Black can do about it. The devilish feature of the position is that if Black tries the plausible *1* .... R–K3 ?? there follows *2* RxR, QxR; *3* N–N7 ch (a *Knight fork*) and Black can resign.

BLACK *to play*

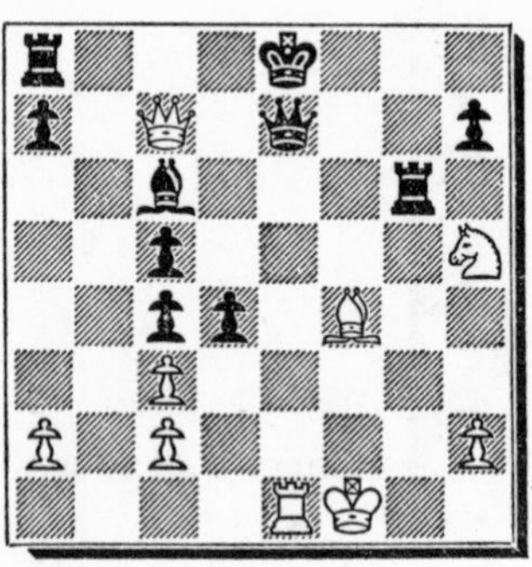

DIAGRAM **119**

WHITE

From what has been said, it is clear that if Black has any resource in this position, it must be uncompromisingly forcing and violent. And so it is!

1 .... R–N8 ch!

A forcing and violent check.

2 KxR QxR mate

A superlatively forcing and violent finish. Moral: be wary about embarking on threats if your own King is not safe.

IN DIAGRAM 120 Black is not menaced in a tactical sense, but his game is apparently lost. He is the Exchange and a Pawn down, and his Queen is *pinned*. As the exchange of Queens is seemingly inevitable, Black must look forward drearily to a hopeless ending. And yet he has a way out!

BLACK *to play*

DIAGRAM 120

WHITE

Only forcing and violent measures can save Black. His only recourse of that kind is a check.

1 .... N–B7 ch!

White's reply is forced, for if 2 RxN ??, Black has 2 .... QxQ ch and wins. White's Rook is tied to the defense of his Queen!

2 K–N1 N–R6 dbl ch

Another forcing, violent move – a *double check*.

3 K–R1 ....

As a matter of fact, White is lucky to have a pin on the Black Queen – otherwise Black could play *3* .... Q–N8 ch!!; *4* RxQ, N–B7 mate!

3	N–B7 ch
4 **K–N1**	N–R6 dbl ch
5 **K–R1**	N–B7 ch

Drawn! White cannot avoid the checks, and Black can continue them forever. In this case, Black's counterthreat was only good enough for a draw – but this is a moral victory under the circumstances.

IN DIAGRAM 121 there is a startling reversal from a position in which Black has a promising attack to a position in which White has a crushing mating attack.

BLACK

DIAGRAM 121

WHITE *to play*

White's King seems somewhat exposed, and Black threatens .... RxP or .... QxNP ch.

But White has an important asset in his powerful Pawn at King Bishop 6. As matters stand, Black's King has no escape and is sadly vulnerable to a mating attack.

1 **R–N4!**	....

A forcing, violent counterthreat. White's chief menace is *2* RxR ch, KxR; *3* Q–N4 ch, K–B1; *4* Q–N7 ch, K–K1; *5* Q–N8 ch, K–Q2; *6* B–N5 ch winning.

If Black tries *1* .... R–Q1 to escape this attack, White's simplest win is the crushing 2 B–B2, winning Black's Queen.

And if Black replies *1* .... RxR, then *2* QxR forces Black to give up a piece by *2* .... QxNP ch to stop 3 Q–N7 mate.

1	**R–KB1**
2 **R–N7**	....

Another forcing, violent threat – this time contemplating 3 RxRP ch! with ensuing checkmate.

Black is helpless in the face of this threat.

2	**RxB**

Now White can win easily enough with 3 RxR, but he prefers the most forcing, violent move of all.

3 **RxRP** ch!	Resigns

For if 3 .... KxR; *4* Q–R5 ch, K–N1; *5* Q–N5 ch, K moves; *6* Q–N7 mate. Every White move has been forcing and violent.

IN POSITIONS where both Kings are menaced, as in Diagram 122, the play is bound to be exciting. The tension is heightened by the mating threats.

BLACK *to play*

DIAGRAM **122**

WHITE

White threatens QxNP mate.

Black can defend with *1* .... R–KN1, but he chooses what he considers a winning move.

1 .... **KR–Q1 ?**

Again the pinning *motif* turns up. It seems that Black must win White's Queen.

However, White can save himself if he seeks forcing, violent moves.

2 **NxR** ....

A forcing, violent move – a capture.

2 .... **RxN**

And now it seems that White's Queen is trapped after all. But now Black is weak on his *inadequately protected first rank,* and White has a winning counterthreat:

3 **R–K8** ch! ....

This move not only releases White's Queen from the *pin;* it actually forces checkmate.

3 .... **RxR**
4 **QxR** mate

FOR OUR last two examples we take positions in which the response to the threat must be of the greatest subtlety. In Diagram 123, for example, Black has a resource which could be discovered only by a grandmaster.

BLACK

DIAGRAM 123

WHITE *to play*

As the position stands, White's position looks distinctly unfavorable. One of his Knights is attacked, and if he plays *1* NPxP, Black replies *1* .... PxP. In that case White is a Pawn down, and his Queen Bishop looks sickly. So White finds a threat that looks very promising.

1 **Q–N3** !? ....

The idea is that on *1* .... PxN White will play 2 P–Q6 dis ch – a *discovered check* that attacks Black's Queen, with consequences that we shall analyze very shortly.

1 .... **PxN** !!

The counterthreat! – a forcing, violent capture. Now White must execute his threat.

2 **P–Q6** dis ch ....

White expects *2* .... Q–B2 (what else?); *3* B–B4. Now Black is in a bad way, as his Queen is *pinned* by White's King Bishop.

If he tries *3* .... N–Q4, he finds himself in a hopeless dilemma after *4* NxN, threatening the fearful *discovered attack 5* N–N6 or *5* N–B7, winning a whole Rook–not to mention the menace of *5* N–K7 ch winning Black's Queen. (*4* .... PxN will not do because of *5* KBxP, winning Black's *pinned* Queen.)

Only an extraordinary move – a forcing, violent move – can save Black. And here it is:

2 .... **B–K3** !!
3 **QxB** ch **Q–B2**

Black has saved the day!

4 **QxQ** ch **RxQ**

Black is not afraid of the pinning move *5* B–B4, for after *5* .... PxN; *6* BxR ch, KxB; *7* BxP he has Bishop and Knight for a Rook – a material advantage which wins for him.

5 **PxP** **R–Q2**

And Black will win the foremost Queen Pawn, leaving him with a Pawn ahead, which is enough to win. Superlative tactics on Black's part!

IN DIAGRAM 124 the play proceeded in a most unfortunate fashion for the defender. Yet if he had found the best defense, he would have escaped unscathed.

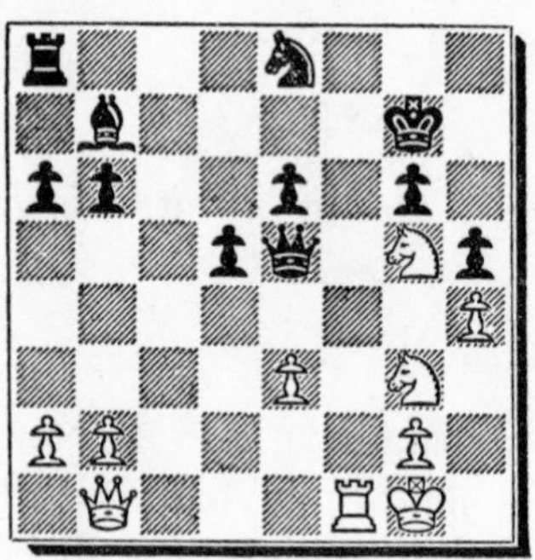

BLACK *to play*

DIAGRAM 124

WHITE

Admittedly, Black's position is difficult.

White threatens *1* R–B7 ch. If then *1* .... K–R3; *2* R–R7 mate. And on other King moves, White plays *2* QxP and Black can resign.

If *1* .... QxN/N6; *2* R–B7 ch wins as just shown.

So, in order to prevent the Rook check, Black played *1* .... N–Q3 ? whereupon *2* NxRP ch! proved decisive in short order (if *2* .... PxN ?; *3* Q–R7 mate).

The right way was:

1 .... N–B3 !

After this move White has a vicious attack that can be parried only by the most skillful play.

2 RxN ! ....

If now *2* .... QxR ?; *3* NxRP ch!, PxN; *4* Q–R7 ch, K–B1; *5*

QxB and White wins easily because of the double threat of *6* QxR and *6* N–R7 ch – a *Knight-forking check* that would win Black's Queen.

2	**KxR!**
3 **Q–KB1 ch**	**K–K2!**

The only move.

4 **Q–B7 ch**	**K–Q3**
5 **QxB**	**QxN/N6!**

Black gives up his Rook – for reasons that will soon become apparent.

6 **QxNP ch**	**K–Q2**
7 **Q–N7 ch**	**K–Q3**
8 **QxR**	**QxKP ch**
9 **K–B1**	**Q–B8 ch**

And now, despite his piece ahead, White cannot win! Black has an endless series of checks from which White's King cannot escape; and so the game is drawn by perpetual check!

With this brilliant example of an outstandingly resourceful counterthreat, we conclude our study of threats. We turn now to a related subject: traps; how they are set, how they work, and how they should be parried.

POSITIONS FOR FURTHER STUDY

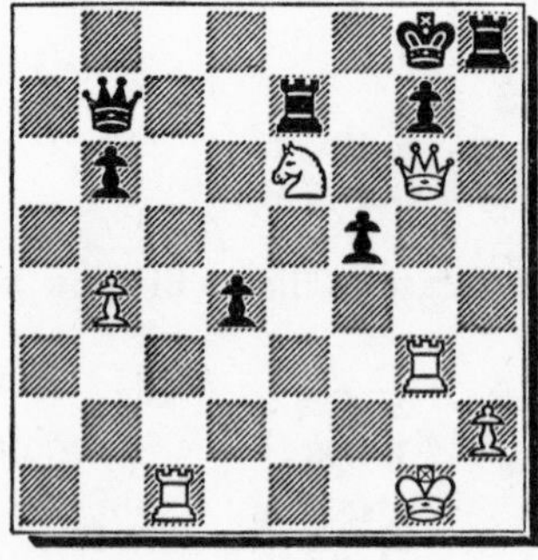

BLACK

DIAGRAM 125

WHITE *to play*

White threatened a mating attack by QxNP ch etc. Against this Black set up an adequate defense by placing his Queen and a Rook on the second rank to defend the threatened point.

Of course, White can win on his material advantage, but he would like to win at once. How can this be done?

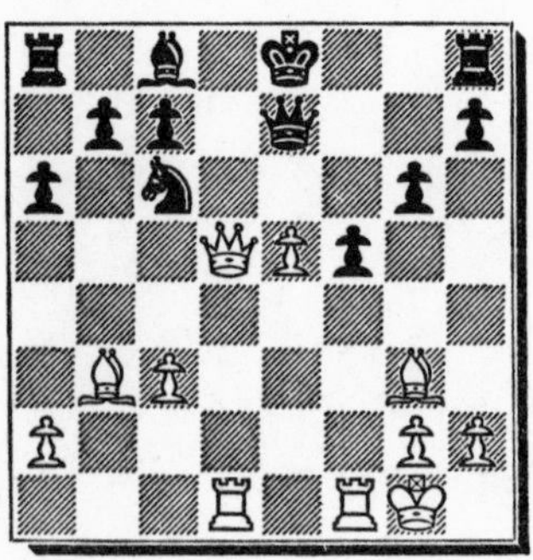

BLACK

DIAGRAM 126

WHITE *to play*

Momentarily Black has adequately defended himself against White's threat of Q–B7 mate. How can White smash Black's defense? Bear in mind that Black's Queen is essential to the defense.

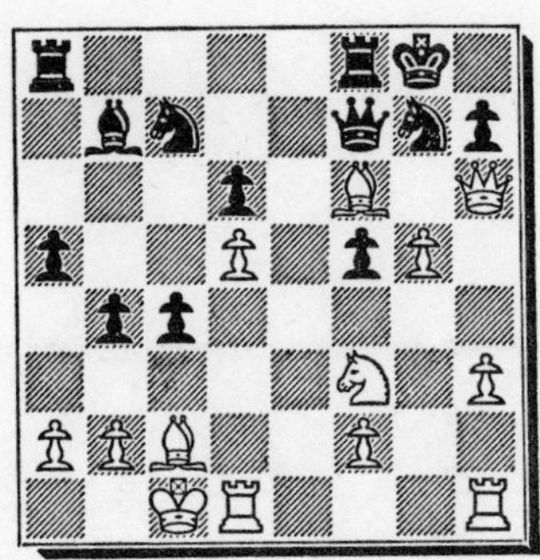

BLACK

DIAGRAM 127

WHITE *to play*

White can play *1* BxN, QxB; *2* QxQP, QR–Q1; *3* Q–QN6, but after 3 . . . . BxP Black would have a splendid position.

White feels there must be something much more forceful at his disposal, and he is right. What should he play?

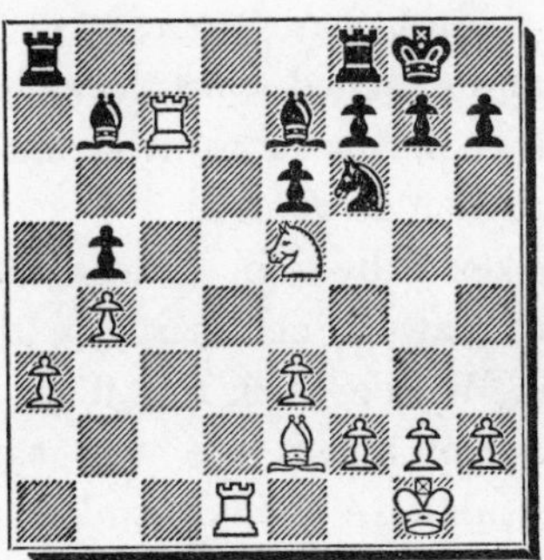

BLACK *to play*

DIAGRAM 128

WHITE

White has given up a piece for a Pawn, and he now expects to regain the piece by his *double attack* on both Black Bishops. Very plausible; but can you find a flaw in his reasoning?

7. *Traps*

"Depend upon it, sir," said Dr. Johnson, "when a man knows he is to be hanged in a fortnight, it concentrates his mind wonderfully."

If this maxim were always valid, nobody would ever succumb to a chess trap. Yet the fact is that chess players are continually falling victim to traps, even the transparent ones.

A trap is an offer with strings attached. One player holds out some attractive bait. The other player snaps at it, and lo and behold! – he loses much more than he gained.

By and large, players are taken in by traps because they overlook the forcing, violent move that will necessarily be the reply to their snatching at the bait. We see, then, that if we concentrate on possible forcing, violent moves, we will manage to avoid traps, be they ever so subtle. *A forcing, violent move is always the mechanism on which a trap depends.*

And, of course, a good trap must have bait–not too plump, of course, for that makes your opponent wary. A Pawn is the ideal bait – enough to interest the prospective victim, and yet not valuable enough to make him too suspicious. This is nicely illustrated in Diagram 129.

White's Queen Bishop Pawn is under attack. To defend it is easy enough, say by *1* P–QN3 or *1* P–B5. Instead White plays:

1 Castles QR! ....

Now Black must ask himself some pertinent questions:

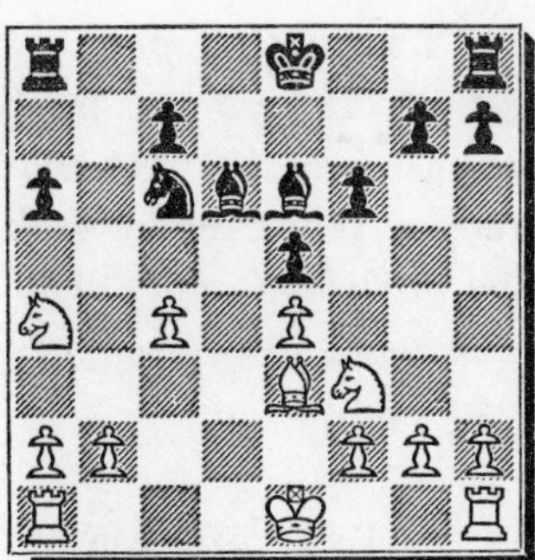

"Why does he leave the Queen Bishop Pawn unguarded? Does he know what he's doing, or is this simply a blunder?"

"How does his last move change the situation from what it was before?"

"If I play .... BxP, does he have some forcing, violent move in reply?"

It really comes down to that last pithy question. (Of course, most players who do not realize the importance of forcing, violent moves never ask themselves that question.)

1 .... **BxP ?**

Black presumably stops, looks, listens, and sees nothing wrong with the capture.

White replies with a forcing, violent capture – a sacrifice of the Exchange.

2 **RxB !** ....

The beauty of this sacrifice of the Exchange is that at first sight it appears quite witless. But there is method in White's seeming madness.

2 .... **PxR**

Naturally forced. But now White has a forcing, violent move – a *Knight fork* – in reply.

3 **N–N6** ....

Simultaneously attacking two unprotected pieces. If Black moves his Bishop, he loses his Rook. If he moves his Rook, he loses his Bishop. Under the circumstances, the best he can do is move his menaced Rook, whereupon White replies *4* NxB, with the winning material advantage of Bishop and Knight against Rook.

IN DIAGRAM 130 White has two ways of winning material. One is quite effective, the other will cost him the game. To decide which is the right way and which is the wrong way, he must consider whether Black has any forcing, violent moves in reply.

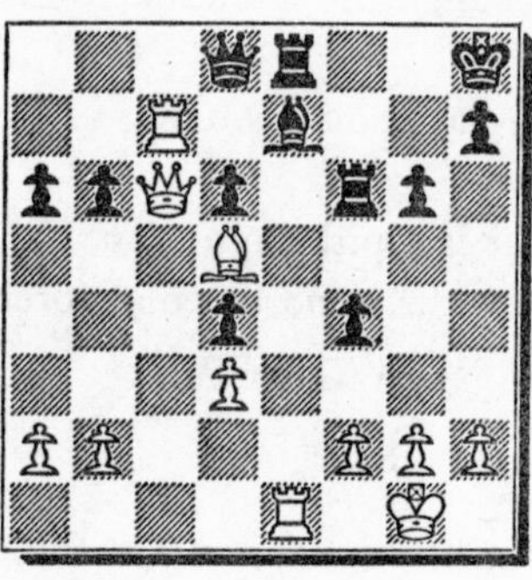

BLACK

DIAGRAM 130

WHITE *to play*

Here is the wrong way for White to play – a very plausible way to go wrong:

1 R/K1xB ? ....

A forcing, violent capture, to be sure. And yet this is just what Black was aiming for.

1 .... RxR
2 R–B8 ? ....

Another forcing, violent move – *pinning* Black's Queen. But it won't do!

2 .... R–K8 mate

This forcing, violent move – exploiting White's *unprotected first rank* – tops White's forcing, violent moves. This was just what Black hoped for.

Here is how White should play to avoid the trap. White attacks Black's Bishop twice, and Black defends it twice. Therefore:

1 **R–Q7!** ....

Driving off Black's Queen from the defense of his Bishop (*remove the guard!*).

1 .... **Q–N1**

Now White can safely capture the Bishop.

2 **R/K1xB** ....

Threatening *3* RxRP mate. One forcing, violent move after another!

2 .... **RxR**
3 **RxR** ....

A new threat: *4* R–K8 ch (*double attack*) winning Black's Queen.

3 .... **R–B1**
4 **Q–Q7** ....

And Black is helpless against the coming RxP mate. White would have won in any event with his extra piece, but heading straight for the mate is of course the quickest way of all.

IN DIAGRAM 131 we see how one tactical slip can transform a win into a loss. White has a terrific initiative and threatens to force the win with *1* R–Q7, driving Black's Queen away for a threefold attack on Black's King Bishop Pawn.

In this desperate situation Black sets a clever trap.

1 .... **QR–Q1 ?!**
2 **RxR** **RxR**

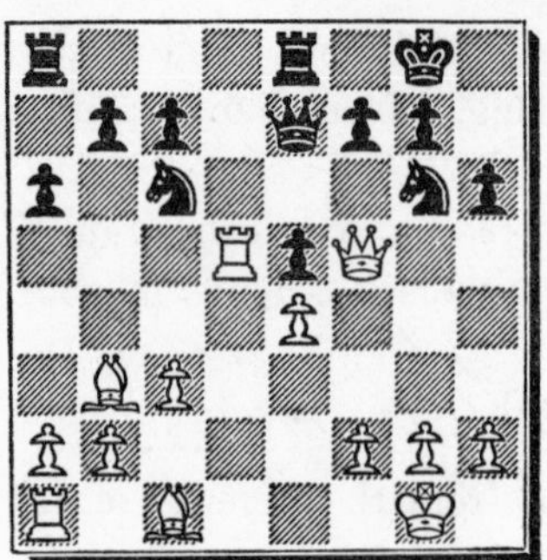

BLACK *to play*

DIAGRAM 131

WHITE

The right way for White to continue is 3 BxRP! winning a clear Pawn. In that event Black dare not reply *3* .... PxB because of *4* QxN ch (Black's King Bishop Pawn is *pinned*) and White wins easily by means of a withering attack.

Instead, White goes astray:

3 **QxN?** ....

Falling into the trap. It is true that Black cannot capture the Queen because his King Bishop Pawn is *pinned*. Nevertheless, White's forcing, violent capture won't work because *he has a tactical weakness in his own camp.*

3 .... **R–Q8** ch!

This forcing, violent check takes advantage of White's *unprotected first rank*. White's Bishop on Knight 3 must capture the obnoxious Rook, whereupon the *pin* on Black's King Bishop Pawn disappears, and Black can capture White's Queen.

4 **BxR** **PxQ**

With a Queen for Rook and Bishop, Black is ahead in material and will win in due course.

IN DIAGRAM 132 we have an amusing series of traps and threats. But White winds up with a mate – which is of course the highest trump of all.

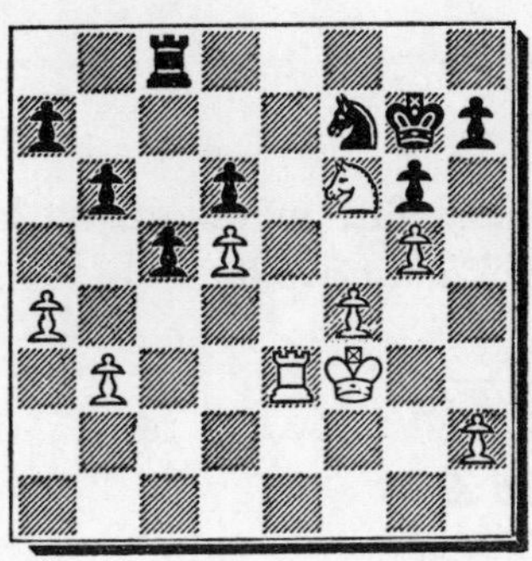

BLACK *to play*

DIAGRAM 132

WHITE

Black's position is very difficult. As matters stand, White is threatening to move his Rook to K7 with powerful pressure on the seventh rank.

Black cannot stop this with *1* .... K–B1, which allows *2* NxP ch. Nor can he stop it with *1* .... R–B2 ? permitting the *Knight forking check* 2 N–K8 ch.

Therefore Black tries a desperate diversion:

1 .... **P–B5 ?!**

Hoping for 2 PxP, RxP which would give him counterplay. Instead, White *pins* the Bishop Pawn.

2 **R–B3 !** ....

Now Black stands to lose a Pawn, as he cannot give his Bishop Pawn any additional support. Therefore he decides on a desperate trap.

2 .... **PxP ?!**

With this forcing, violent move Black plays to queen a Pawn.

3 **RxR !** **P–N7**

Carrying out his idea. Black's Pawn has a clear road to promotion, but White has a forcing, violent move – a checkmate!

4 **R–KN8** mate

Black's trap failed because White had a superior tactical resource.

IN DIAGRAM 133 White's first move sets no less than three traps, all of which Black must avoid!

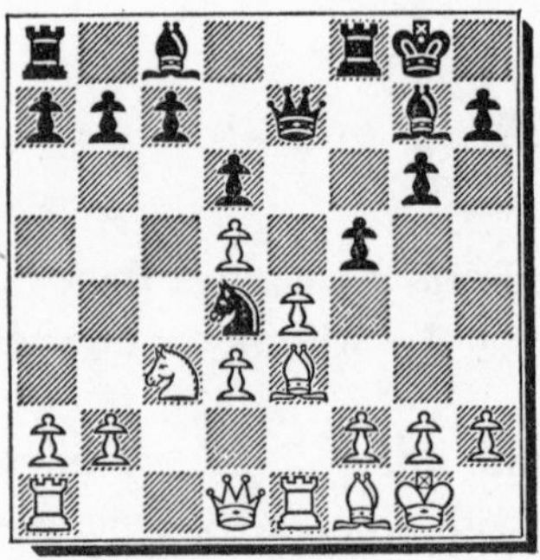

BLACK

DIAGRAM 133

WHITE *to play*

White sets his traps with:

1 **P–K5!** ....

This move looks nonsensical, as Black can capture the King Pawn three different ways. But each method loses:

1 .... PxP? will not do because in that case *2* BxN wins a piece, as Black's King Pawn is *pinned.*

1 .... BxP? is equally unavailing, for *2* BxN still wins a piece, as Black's King Bishop is *pinned.*

Even *1* .... QxP? will not do, for then *2* B–N5! (*discovered attack*) wins Black's Queen.

Meanwhile Black must protect his menaced Knight.

1	**P–B4**
2 **P–K6**	....

And White has a marked positional advantage with his far advanced, protected passed Pawn.

Here we make an interesting observation: White used his forcing, violent first move to obtain a positional advantage. This often happens as the result of a trappy move which tempts the opponent without harming one's own position.

IN DIAGRAM 134 White sets two traps. One is sound, the other has a flaw. In the latter case, however, White is able to preserve equality.

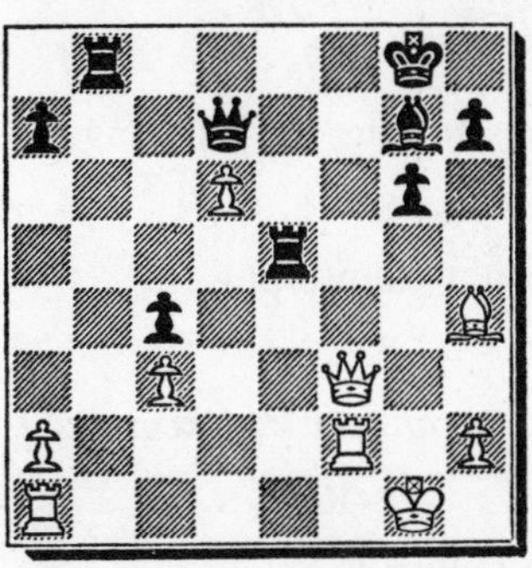

BLACK

DIAGRAM 134

WHITE *to play*

White sets his traps with:

1 QR–KB1 !? ....

Suppose Black, alarmed by the concentration of White's forces on the open King Bishop file, plays:

1 .... R–KB1 ?

In that case White plays a series of forcing, violent checks to ensure the queening of his advanced passed Pawn, thus:

2 QxR ch!	BxQ
3 RxB ch	K–N2
4 R/B1–B7 ch	QxR
5 RxQ ch	KxR

Now Black is the Exchange ahead, but the following move reveals that he has fallen into a trap.

6 P–Q7 ! ....

After this, Black must part with his Rook.

6 .... R–Q4
7 P–Q8/Q RxQ
8 BxR ....

With a whole piece to the good, White wins effortlessly. This is a typical, instructive queening maneuver.

Now let us see the fate of White's other trap (from Diagram 134):

1 QR–KB1 !? QxP
2 B–N3 ....

With this *pin* White expects to win the Exchange.

2 .... R–N4

Black extricates himself with a counterpin.

3 K–R1 ....

White in turn unpins his Bishop and threatens BxQ.

3 .... B–K4

Parrying the attack on his Queen.

4 BxB RxB
5 Q–B7 ch K–R1
6 QxBP Q–Q4 ch
7 QxQ RxQ

With a draw as the likely outcome.

This trap had paradoxical consequences. The safe-looking defense would have lost; the risky-looking defense turned out to be safe.

IN DIAGRAM 135 Black carelessly falls into an obvious trap which he could have turned to his advantage with proper play.

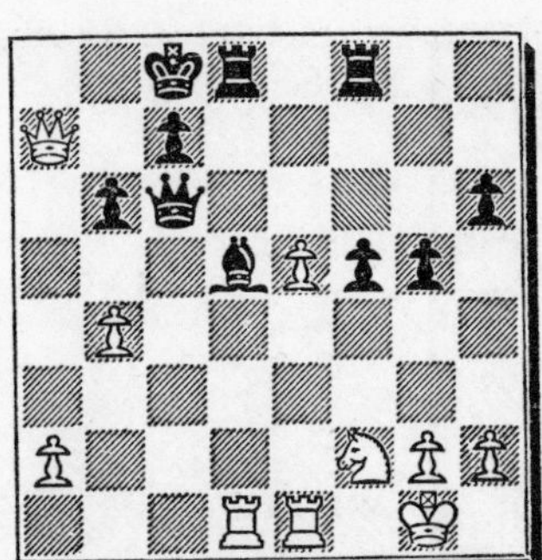

White baits the trap with:

1 **P–K6**?! ....

A forcing, violent move threatening *2* P–K7 (*double attack*). However, Black can repulse the attack easily with *1* .... KR–K1, after which the loss of White's King Pawn is only a matter of time.

1 .... **BxKP**?
2 **R–QB1**! ....

A forcing, violent move which attacks Black's Queen.

2 .... **Q–Q3**

Black's Queen is an *overworked piece*—it has to prevent QxBP mate or RxP mate, and it also has to guard the Black Bishop.

3 **RxB** ....

Black dare not reply 3 .... QxR which would allow mate on the move. Thus White has won a piece, which gives him an easy win.

IN DIAGRAM 136 White succumbs to an obvious trap because he does not realize the strength of forcing, violent moves.

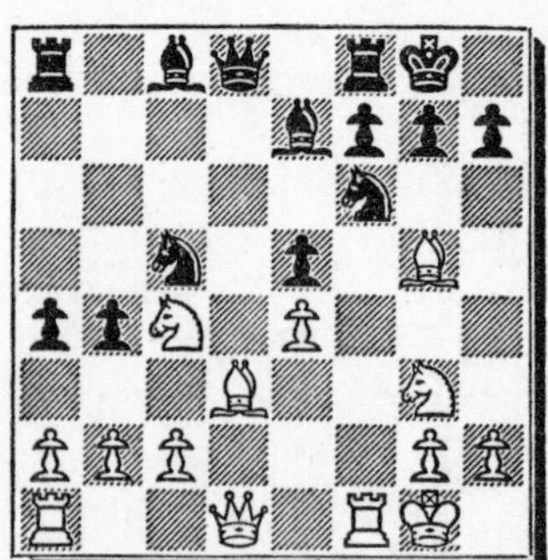

DIAGRAM 136

Black's King Pawn is attacked. Instead of defending it, he calmly plays:

1 .... **B–K3**!

Ignoring the attack on his King Pawn.

Now White should examine the position with a critical eye to ascertain whether Black's King Pawn is indirectly protected by some forcing, violent move. Failing to do this, he plays:

2 **NxP**? **Q–Q5** ch!

Black gives check and simultaneously attacks White's exposed Knight (*double attack*).

3 **K–R1** **QxN**

Black has won a piece, and should win easily.

IN DIAGRAM 137 White also makes good use of an indirect defense based on a mating threat. Black fails to discover the reason for White's generosity.

White's Queen Rook Pawn is doubly attacked, and only defended once. At his last move White played a Rook from Queen 1 to Queen 7, instead of lending additional protection to his menaced Queen Rook Pawn. Failing to see any forcing, violent move for his opponent, Black foolishly plays:

BLACK *to play*

DIAGRAM 137

WHITE

---

1	RxRP ??
2 RxR	RxR
3 R–Q8 ch!	....

A forcing, violent threat against Black's *unprotected first rank.*

3	B–B1
4 B–R6	....

With this *pin* White leaves Black helpless against the threat of RxB mate.

IN DIAGRAM 138 White uses a trap to enforce a useful strategical idea.

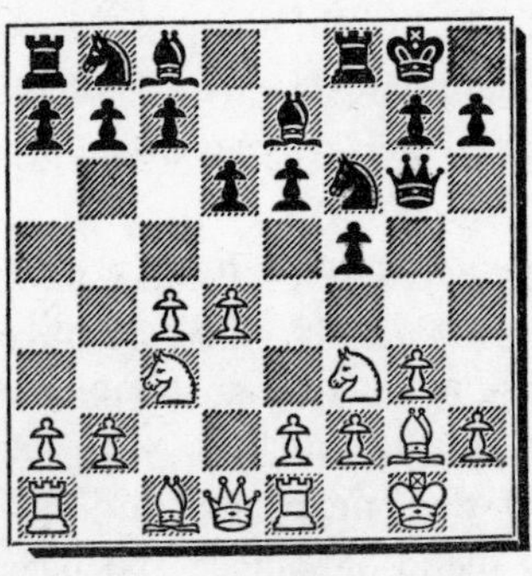

BLACK

DIAGRAM 138

WHITE *to play*

White wants to play P–K4, which would greatly increase his command of the board by giving his pieces more scope. But White has only two pieces trained on his King 4 square, while Black has three pieces aiming at that square. It therefore follows that P–K4 is impossible.

At least it is impossible according to conventional reasoning which would be sound in 99 cases out of a hundred. But that conventional reasoning does not apply here, *because White has a forcing, violent resource at his command.*

This is how the trap unfolds:

1 **P–K4!**	**PxP**
2 **NxP!**	....

White is very sure of himself. To all intents and purposes, he is giving up a piece.

2	**NxN**
3 **RxN!**	....

And now he gives up a whole Rook! Without looking any further into the motives for this suspicious generosity, Black grabs:

3	**QxR?**
4 **N–R4!**	....

Attacking the Black Queen and winning her, as she has no flight square.

One last point: Suppose that, at move three, Black had had the good sense not to snap at the Rook. Could we then say that the trap had been a failure? No, for although in that case the trap would not achieve its maximum objective, it would result in the freeing of White's game, which was his other purpose in setting the trap.

In this chapter we have seen that traps form a very important part of tactical play. They may save a lost game from disaster; they may speed up an already won game; they may completely unnerve a player who has an easy win; and in all cases they lend that touch of the unexpected and unforeseen that makes chess a delightful blend of science and hazard.

POSITIONS FOR FURTHER STUDY

BLACK *to play*

DIAGRAM 139

WHITE

Black sees that he can win a Pawn by playing *1* .... Q–N3 threatening *2* .... BxP ch and also *2* .... QxP.

In reply to *1* .... Q–N3 White calmly plays 2 Castles, guarding his King Bishop Pawn but leaving his Queen Knight Pawn undefended. In so doing, White is setting a trap for Black.

To sum up: after *1* .... Q–N3; 2 Castles, is 2 .... QxP advisable for Black, or should he avoid that move?

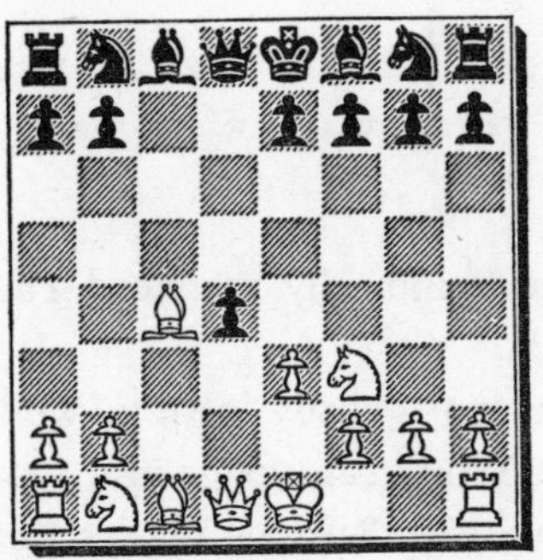

BLACK *to play*

DIAGRAM 140

WHITE

Black sees that he can win a Pawn by *1* .... PxP. Is that capture advisable for him?

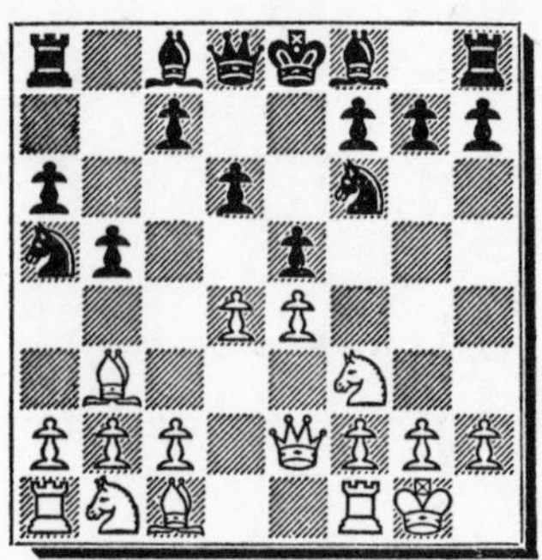

BLACK *to play*

DIAGRAM 141

WHITE

White threatens to win a Pawn by playing PxP and then answering Black's reply .... PxP with NxP.

Consequently, in the position of Diagram 141, Black plays *1* .... B–N5 *pinning* White's King Knight. Black reasons that the pin will prevent White from winning a Pawn. Is Black right or wrong?

BLACK *to play*

DIAGRAM 142

WHITE

Black wants to regain his temporarily sacrificed Pawn and therefore plays *1* .... NxQBP.

In order to decide if this move is really feasible, we have to ask ourselves whether or not White can now win a piece by *2* BxN ch, PxB; *3* QxB – or even *2* QxB (since Black's Knight on Queen Bishop 3 is *pinned*).

What is your answer to these questions?

8. *How to Win Material*

At this point we return to the theme of Chapter 3 – that superior force must win.

In the last four chapters we have seen how forcing, violent moves – checks, captures, and all the other kinds – can win material. In this last chapter we want to review this vital theme, but with a change of emphasis.

Whereas in the earlier chapters we stressed *tactical methods* – mate threats, Knight forks, etc. – we are now interested in one specific facet of these methods – how they are used to win material.

Another important feature of this chapter is that we shall try to appraise each position in terms of its most significant factor. You will soon realize that this type of examination is a sure guide to decisive action.

In Diagram 143, for example, the salient feature which immediately catches our attention is that Black's King Pawn and Knight Pawn are weak. *Neither of these Pawns is protected by a Pawn,* and consequently they must be protected by pieces. Such Pawns are ideal targets for hostile threats.

You can always tell a good chessplayer by the incisive way he fastens on a vulnerable target. Thus White has one Rook trained on the weak Knight Pawn. (Observe that this ties down a Black Rook to the defense.)

Now White introduces a new threat:

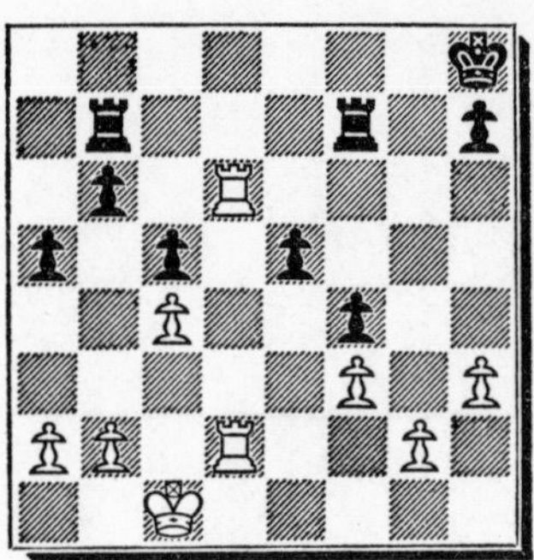

BLACK

DIAGRAM 143

WHITE *to play*

---

1 R–K2 ....

If now *1* .... R–B4, White replies 2 R–K6 – still another new threat – winning the weak King Pawn.

1 .... R/B2–K2
2 R–Q5 ....

White attacks the King Pawn twice. It is defended only once, and Black cannot bring up any more defensive reserves. So White wins the King Pawn, which should assure him a winning endgame.

THIS WAS a simple but superlative study in the art of bringing pressure to bear on a weakness by means of cumulative threats.

In Diagram 144, however, a different technique is required. Black's three pieces can conduct a concentrated attack, whereas White's pieces are scattered.

Studying this position, we realize that White's Queen is tied to the defense of the White Bishop. At the same time, White's Queen must keep an eye on the possibility of .... Q–B8 ch.

True, Black is already a Pawn ahead and can win a second

BLACK *to play*

DIAGRAM 144

WHITE

Pawn by .... BxP. But the precarious position of White's pieces suggests the theme of *remove the guard.* Therefore:

1 .... Q–B8 ch!

This forcing, violent check decides the game at once.

If 2 QxQ, RxQ ch; 3 K–R2, B–B5 ch! winning the White Rook in addition to the White Bishop!

If 2 K–R2, B–B5 ch is murderous. Thus Black wins quickly by taking advantage of the awkward disposition of White's pieces.

IN DIAGRAM 145, White is a Pawn ahead and wants to increase his material advantage.

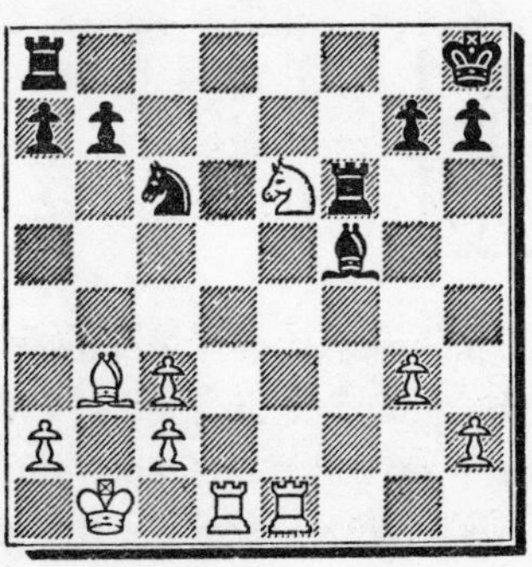

BLACK

DIAGRAM 145

WHITE *to play*

White sees that he can win another Pawn by attacking on Black's *vulnerable first rank.*

1 **N–Q8!** ....

This forcing, violent threat attacks Black's Queen Knight Pawn and also threatens *2* R–K8 ch, R–B1; *3* RxR mate.

Note that *1* .... NxN ?? will not do because of *2* R–K8 ch, R–B1; *3* RxR mate.

Nor is *1* .... RxN ?? any better because of *2* RxR ch, NxR; *3* R–K8 ch, R–B1; *4* RxR mate.

1 .... **R–KB1**
2 **NxP** ....

And White has gained a second Pawn, which should assure him a winning endgame.

IN DIAGRAM 146 the presence of the White King and a Black Bishop on the same diagonal suggests the possibility of *double attack* with check.

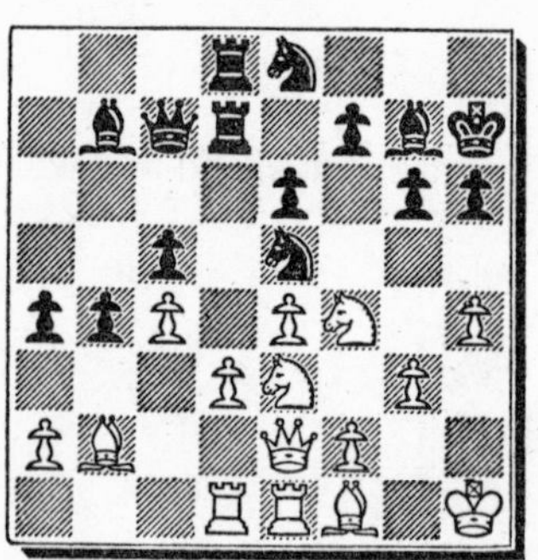

BLACK *to play*

DIAGRAM **146**

WHITE

White's Queen Pawn is a weakness because it cannot be protected by a Pawn and must be guarded by pieces. (We dealt with the same theme in Diagram 143.) It seems snugly defended, however, for though it is attacked by three Black pieces, it is defended by four White pieces. Nevertheless, thanks to the fact that Black's Queen Bishop is on *the same diagonal* with White's King, Black has a startling sacrifice:

1 .... NxQP !

A forcing, violent capture.

2 NxN ....

Has Black simply lost a piece?

No, for Black has another forcing, violent move – a *double attack* with check.

2 .... BxP ch
3 P–B3 BxN

Thus Black regains the sacrificed piece and remains two Pawns ahead. This should win the game for him.

THE SITUATION in Diagram 147 seems highly favorable for White, as he is a Pawn ahead and is also attacking a Black Rook. Yet Black knows how to make clever use of his extra mobility.

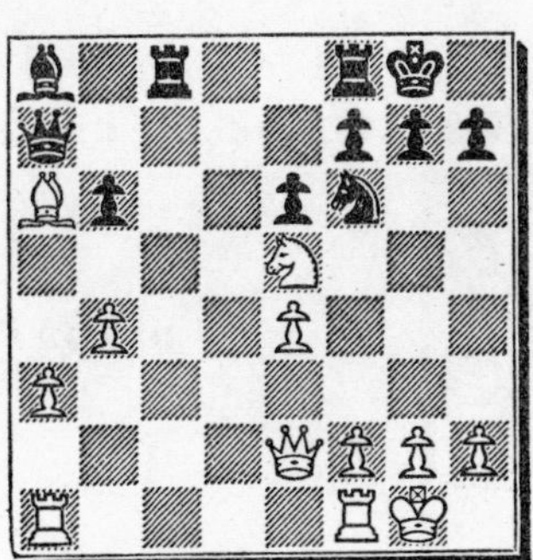

BLACK *to play*

DIAGRAM 147

WHITE

Black's next move should result in the regain of his Pawn, and may yield more.

1 .... R–B6 !

White has to keep an eye on his wandering Bishop, and he also has to find a defense for his King Pawn, which is doubly attacked.

His safest course is *2* B–Q3, RxP; *3* RxR, QxR; *4* P–N5 with equal chances. Instead, he goes wildly wrong with an apparently solid move which actually leaves him wide open to attack.

2 **P–B3 ??** ....

This opens up the diagonal extending from the White King to the Black Queen. How can Black turn this to advantage?

2 .... **P–QN4** dis ch!

This *discovered check* menaces White's King and at the same time shuts off the White Queen's protection of the White Bishop. After White gets his King out of danger, Black continues *3* .... QxB, with an easy win as he is a piece up.

SO GREAT is Black's pressure in Diagram 148 that White is helpless. Black's immediate threat is .... BxR, winning the Exchange.

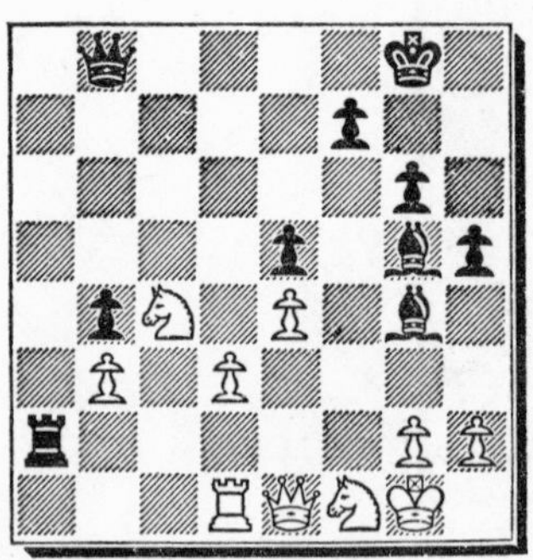

BLACK

DIAGRAM **148**

WHITE *to play*

White must move his attacked Rook – but where? If *1* R–Q2, Black replies *1* .... BxR, winning the Exchange.

On *1* R–B1 there follows *1* .... R–K7! threatening White's Queen, and if *2* Q–Q1 Black has *2* .... RxNP ch (*discovered attack* with check) winning White's Queen.

Most interesting is the sequence of forcing, violent moves unleashed by Black after *1* R–N1: *1* .... R–K7; *2* Q–N3, B–B5; *3* Q–R4, P–N4! trapping White's Queen in broad daylight.

So White plays a move which loses at once, though it can hardly be called a blunder.

1 **R–R1** **Q–R2 ch!**

Double attack with check. Black wins a Rook with this check.

In such positions, when threats flourish on all parts of the board, it is reasonable to expect some substantial gain of material as a result of the pressure.

IN DIAGRAM 149 White's Rooks are doubled on the King file, and the White Knight which masks that file is in a position to play a forcing, violent check. This suggests a powerful stroke to White.

BLACK

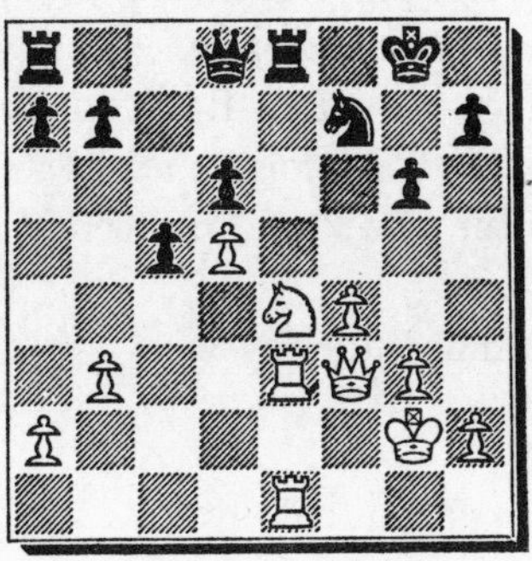

DIAGRAM 149

WHITE *to play*

To make use of his control of the King file and the possibility of a *Knight-forking check,* White resorts to a *discovered attack:*

1 **N–B6 ch!** **QxN**

Forced.

2	RxR ch	RxR
3	RxR ch	....

Having won the Exchange, White should win the endgame with little difficulty.

An interesting study in *double attack* and *counterthreat* turns up in Diagram 150.

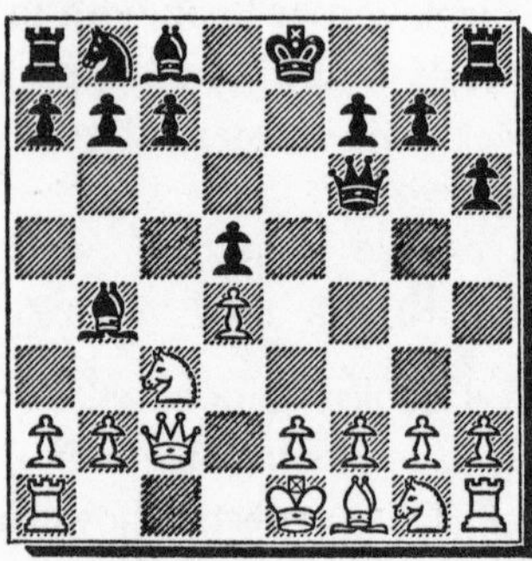

BLACK

DIAGRAM 150

WHITE *to play*

Black threatens .... QxQP. White can defend easily enough with P–K3, but this is too uninspired for him.

On the other hand, the aggressive *1* Q–R4 ch (*double attack* with check) leads to nothing, as Black has an adequate reply in *1* .... N–B3, interposing to the check and protecting his menaced Bishop.

White therefore bides his time and plays:

1	P–QR3	....

Attacking Black's King Bishop, so that after *1* .... BxN ch he can reply *2* PxB or *2* QxB guarding his Queen Pawn.

1	....	B–KB4?

Instead of meeting the threat head-on, Black plays a forcing, violent threat (attack on White's Queen). But he overlooks that

White's Queen can flee and at the same time deliver a forcing, violent *double attack* with check.

2 Q–R4 ch ....

Since Black is in check, he has no time to save his menaced Bishop. And 2 .... N–B3 will no longer do, as his King Bishop is attacked not only by White's Queen but also by his Queen Rook Pawn.

And so, no matter how Black plays, he loses his King Bishop.

Black was seriously at fault in not reckoning with the consequences of an available check.

A DOUBLE ATTACK with check plays a double role in Diagram 151. The first of these double attacks is easy to see, whereas the second is difficult to see, primarily because White's Queen attacks in divergent directions.

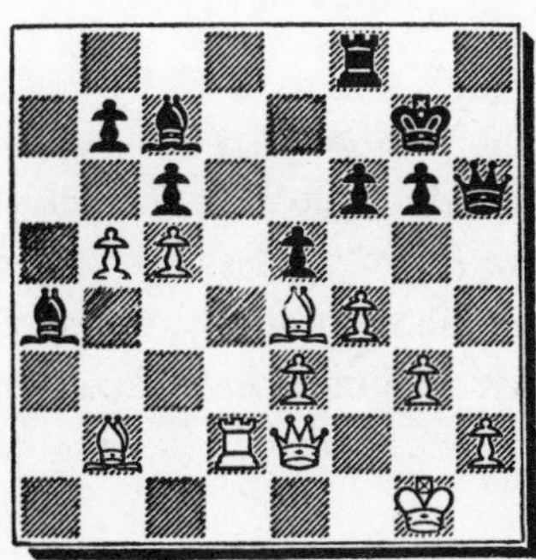

DIAGRAM 151

This position is perfect for a little lecture on how you find opportunities for winning material. Always on the lookout for forcing, violent moves, you note that (*a*) both Black Bishops are unprotected and that (*b*) White has a *double attack* with check by R–Q7 ch.

It is true that the Rook check does not win of and by itself. But our guiding thought throughout this book has been that if you seek out the forcing, violent moves, success will come to you almost automatically. And that thought is borne out by the play that follows from Diagram 151.

1 **R–Q7** ch ....

This forcing, violent move is obvious – and very powerful as well.

1 .... **R–B2**

The only move to save his threatened Bishop. How does White proceed? He needs another forcing, violent move – this time a *check*. And this move is quite obvious too.

2 **RxR** ch **KxR**

Again Black's reply is forced.

Now one more *double attack* with check. White has already created the perfect setting.

3 **Q–B4** ch **K** moves
4 **QxB** ....

Mission accomplished – White has an easy win with a piece ahead. One more element should be noticed – *Black's Queen was far away at the side of the board,* useless for protective or defensive purposes. As we have seen repeatedly, the player with the more active Queen is always in a most favorable position to achieve his objective.

FEW PLAYERS realize that mate threats can turn up even in quite simple positions where the material on both sides has been drastically reduced. This is neatly illustrated in Diagram 152.

Black begins with a threat which can be easily parried – or so it seems.

1 .... **R–KN7**!

BLACK *to play*

DIAGRAM 152

WHITE

Attacking White's Knight Pawn, which cannot be defended. But White does have a counterthreat.

2 **P–R4** ....

If now 2 .... PxP ??; 3 NxP ch winning the Black Rook with a *Knight-forking check.*

And if 2 .... RxP; 3 PxP and White has avoided loss of material.

2 .... **P–N5 !**

A forcing, violent move: he keeps White's Knight Pawn under surveillance, and at the same time attacks his Knight.

White has only one way out – a forcing, violent *check.*

3 **N–K5 ch** **K–B3**

Still keeping White's Knight Pawn under attack. But now White has a defense – or so he thinks.

4 **K–B4** **R–K7 !!**

A baleful forcing, violent move – a mate threat. To prevent .... R–K5 mate, White must give up a piece.

4 **NxNP ch** **PxN**

With a piece for a Pawn, Black has an easy endgame win.

IT TAKES only the most cursory glance at Diagram 153 to see that Black's Rook at King Bishop 3 is an *overworked piece.* For this Rook must guard the other Black Rook, and must also protect the Black Knight.

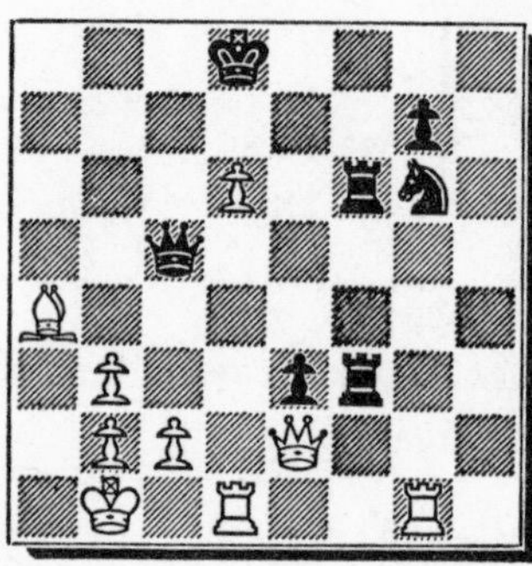

BLACK

DIAGRAM 153

WHITE *to play*

White seeks a forcing, violent move:

1 **RxN!** ....

So that if *1* ....RxR?; *2* QxR and White has won a piece. But Black has a malicious counterthreat.

1 .... **R–B7**

Keeping White's Rook under attack and attacking his Queen as well. White finds the strongest reply.

2 **RxR!** ....

This forcing, violent move involves a *mate threat.* If *2* .... RxQ; *3* R–B8 mate! As usual, a mate threat tops all other threats.

2 .... **PxR**
3 **Q–Q3** Resigns

White's material advantage wins easily for him.

DISCOVERED ATTACKS play a star role in the play that evolves from Diagram 154. The dominating motif is the presence of Black's Queen and White's Queen Bishop on the long diagonal, coupled with the possibility of unmasking checks by the Black Knights.

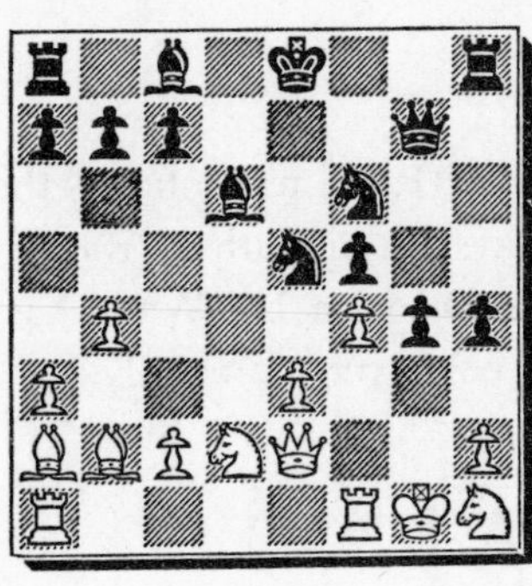

BLACK *to play*

DIAGRAM 154

WHITE

Black's attacked Knight must be saved – but how? By a forcing, violent move.

1 .... **N–B6** ch!

For if 2 NxN, PxN dis ch with a *discovered check* that wins White's Queen!

If instead 2 K–B2, NxN ! (the simplest); 3 QxN, N–K5 ch with a *discovered attack* that wins White's Queen Bishop. Or 3 BxN, N–K5 ch! – a *Knight-forking check* which likewise leaves Black a piece ahead.

2 **K–N2** **P–R6** ch!

If now 3 K–N3, NxN ! wins a piece as in the previous variation – or simply 2 .... N–R4 ch with *discovered attack.*

This forcing, violent move compels White's King to move to a square on which disaster awaits him.

3 **K–B2** **NxN**

If now 4 BxN, N–K5 ch! wins a piece for Black.

4 **QxN** **N–K5** ch

A *discovered attack* with check!

5 **K–N1** **QxB**

And with a piece ahead, Black is assured of victory.

Black harmoniously combined various types of forcing, violent moves – checks, captures, and discovered attacks – to win a decisive amount of material.

IT STANDS TO REASON that Pawn promotion – the greatest material gain of all – plays an important role in many stratagems to win material. In Diagram 155 White has an opportunity to demonstrate this point very forcefully.

BLACK

DIAGRAM **155**

WHITE *to play*

This position is a fine example of the view that familiarity with forcing, violent moves helps us to select the strongest move in any given position.

White is the Exchange ahead; he is ahead in material. But such an endgame can take twenty or thirty moves to win. In order to win quickly, we must realize that White has a passed Pawn on the seventh rank. This suggests the theme of *Pawn promotion* to us.

True, Black's blockading Bishop prevents the Queen Pawn from queening. This suggests to us the need for a forcing, violent move to thrust the Bishop out of the way. The right move for this purpose is:

1 **R–K1!** ....

This forcing, violent move prevents Black's King from approaching the Queen Pawn. It also prepares for 2 R–K8, attacking the Bishop. Then, when the Bishop moves out of attacking range, White queens his Pawn. Here is a sample continuation:

1	P–B4
2 R–K8	B–N3
3 P–Q8/Q	....

Naturally Black cannot allow this Queen to remain on the board.

3	BxQ
4 RxB	....

A typical queening operation. With a whole Rook ahead, White wins effortlessly.

SOMETIMES a Pawn promotion can be engineered only with the help of other themes. In such cases we must not be afraid of heavy sacrifices which are minor in comparison to the greater good of promoting a Pawn to a Queen. This is exemplified in Diagram 156.

BLACK *to play*

DIAGRAM 156

WHITE

Black is naturally eager to queen his King Pawn, a far advanced passed Pawn. But if he impetuously advances *1* ....

P–K7? White replies 2 K–B2, R–K4 (threatening to queen); 3 K–K1! with an unassailable blockade.

Obviously, this won't do. Black must invoke the familiar principle of the forcing, violent move.

1 .... **R–R8** ch!

This stamps White's King as an *overworked piece*. He must prevent the Pawn from queening, but, more important, he *must get out of check*. And there is only one way to do it.

2 **KxR** ....

But now White's King can no longer stop the Pawn from queening.

2 .... **P–K7**
3 **P–N3** ch ....

A last try. Perhaps Black will blunder and play 3 .... K–N5? or 3 .... K–N4? or 3 .... K–B4? or 3 .... K–K4? allowing White's Rook to reach the King 3 square – and win!

3 .... **K–K5**!

After this move, neither the White King nor the White Rook can stop Black's King Pawn from becoming a Queen. And with Queen against Rook, Black will have an overwhelming material advantage.

THE MANNER in which White utilizes the theme of Pawn promotion in Diagram 157 is nothing short of astounding. He already has a far advanced passed Pawn, but cannot accomplish anything with it. So he gives up that Pawn in order to get another passed Pawn against which Black is helpless!

White begins with a forcing, violent threat: *double attack* by means of a Pawn fork.

1 **P–Q7** ch! **KxP**

The only move. Now White plays a second forcing, violent move: a *double attack* with check.

2 **RxBP ch**	**K–K1**
3 **RxRP**	**....**

White has achieved his objective: he has a new passed Pawn which is outside the reach of Black's pieces.

And White has a forcing, violent threat: *4* R–R8 ch, K–Q2; *5* RxR, KxR; *6* P–R7 and there is no way for Black to stop the Pawn from queening!

3 **....**	**RxP**

This parries White's threat momentarily.

4 **K–Q3 !**	**....**

Attacking Black's Rook and protecting his Knight. Black has no good move left, for example:

4 .... R–B1; *5* R–R8 ch, K–Q2; *6* RxR, KxR; *7* P–R7 and the passed Pawn queens.

Or *4* .... B–Q4; *5* R–N7 !, K–B1 (to stop P–R7); *6* R–KB1 ch, K–K1; *7* P–R7, and the passed Pawn queens.

Or *4* .... R–R5; *5* R–N7, K–B1 (to stop P–R7); *6* NxP ch, K–K1; *7* P–R7 and the passed Pawn queens.

Black resigns, as he is helpless.

AS WE HAVE seen, *double attack* is a favorite technique for gaining material. We see it used to remarkable advantage in our final example, in Diagram 158.

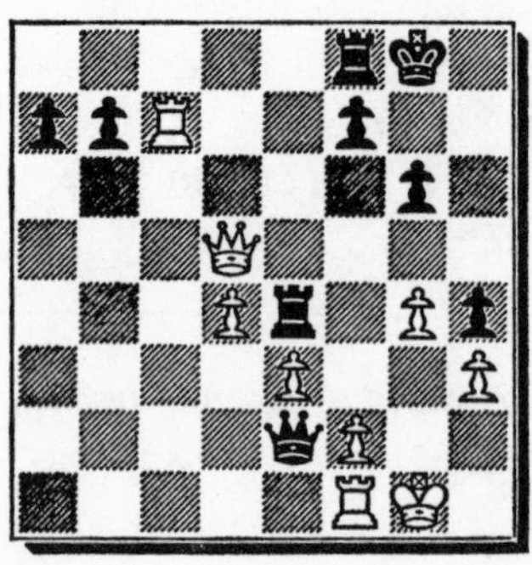

BLACK *to play*

DIAGRAM 158

WHITE

Black's Rook on King 5 is attacked. In fact, White has a *double attack* on this Rook and on Black's Queen Knight Pawn. Apparently the Rook must retreat, after which White will pick up the Queen Knight Pawn. Only a forcing, violent move can save Black.

And Black finds the resource he needs in an amazing move:

1	**RxKP !!**

The soundness of this move rests on the fact that White's Rook on Queen Bishop 7 is *unprotected.* For example: 2 PxR, QxKP ch; 3 R–B2 (if 3 K–R2 or 3 K–N2, Q–KN6 ch wins the distant Rook by *double attack;* or 3 K–R1, QxRP ch; 4 K–N1, Q–KN6 ch with the same result), Q–KN6 ch again winning White's far-off Rook.

And if 2 RxNP, RxP; 3 RxRP, QxNP ch and Black wins because of his material advantage and the exposed state of White's King.

2 **Q–N2**	**R–QN6**
3 **RxNP**	**RxR**
4 **QxR**	**Q–Q6 !**

Another *double attack.*

5 **QxRP** **QxRP**

After this Black has the win well in hand. For example: *6* Q–Q7 (to protect his Knight Pawn), Q–KB6 (threatening .... P–R6 followed by .... Q–N7 mate); *7* K–R2, P–R6 (threatening .... Q–N7 mate); *8* R–KN1, QxBP ch; *9* K–R1, Q–B6 ch; *10* K–R2, R–R1! with the deadly threat of .... R–R7 ch forcing checkmate.

BLACK

DIAGRAM 159

WHITE *to play*

6 **P–B3** **Q–N6 ch**
7 **K–R1** **R–K1**

With the terrible mate threat of .... R–K7 etc.

8 **Q–R2** **R–K8!**

Another forcing, violent move: if *9* RxR, QxR ch; *10* K–R2, Q–N6 ch; *11* K–R1, QxBP ch; *12* K–R2, QxP and Black has an easy win because of his material advantage.

9 **Q–KN2** ....

Justified despair. After the ensuing exchanges, Black will win the King and Pawn ending despite the fact that material is even!

9 .... **QxQ ch**
10 **KxQ** **RxR**
11 **KxR** **P–N4!**
12 **K–B2** **K–B1**

Black's new threat: to bring his King to Queen 4, attacking White's isolated Queen Pawn. Sooner or later White must renounce his King's protection of this Pawn, because of the passed Rook Pawn's *promotion threat.* Thus, although material is even, White is helpless against Black's threat to win the Queen Pawn.

13 **K–K3**	**K–K2**

Now White cannot play *14* K–K4? or *14* K–Q3?, for then comes *14* .... P–R6 and the Rook Pawn queens, as it is beyond the reach of White's King. White's King must be ready to pounce on the passed Rook Pawn.

14 **K–K2**	**K–Q3**
15 **K–B2**	**K–Q4**
16 **K–K3**	**K–B5!**

This wins the Queen Pawn, for on *17* K–K4 Black forces the game with *17* .... P–R6 etc.

17 **K–B2**	**KxP**
18 **K–K2**	**P–B3!**
19 **K–B2**	**K–Q6**
20 **K–N2**	**K–K7**

White resigns, as he is helpless against Black's threat to win the two remaining White Pawns.

Thus we conclude our study of forcing, violent moves. Time and again we have seen how the intensive search leads to a win in positions that might otherwise thoroughly baffle the ordinary player. Forcing, violent moves give purpose and plan to our play; they illuminate many an obscure position; they enable us to smash our opponent's resistance and achieve victory in the quickest, most effective way. They make us much better chessplayers than we could ever become in any other way.

POSITIONS FOR FURTHER STUDY

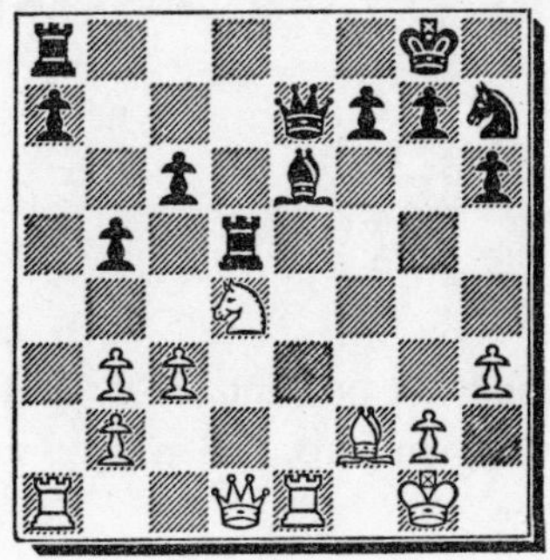

BLACK

DIAGRAM 160

WHITE *to play*

White is a Pawn down, and in order to regain the lost material, he naturally plays:

1 NxBP! ....

If now *1* .... RxQ there follows *2* NxQ ch, K–B1; *3* KRxR, KxN; *4* RxP ch and White, with the Exchange and a Pawn to the good, has an easy win.

1 .... Q–Q2

Black attacks the Knight while still keeping White's Queen under attack. White can extricate himself safely with 2 N–Q4. But this is rather colorless, giving rise to the question of whether he has a stronger second move. What do you think?

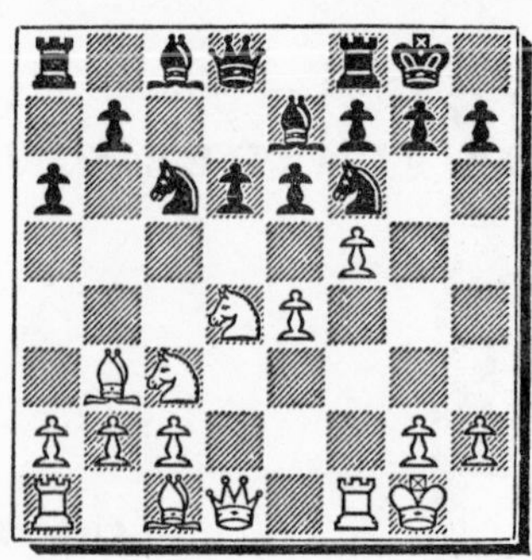

BLACK *to play*

DIAGRAM 161

WHITE

White has seriously weakened his position. How can Black take advantage of this weakening to force the win of substantial material?

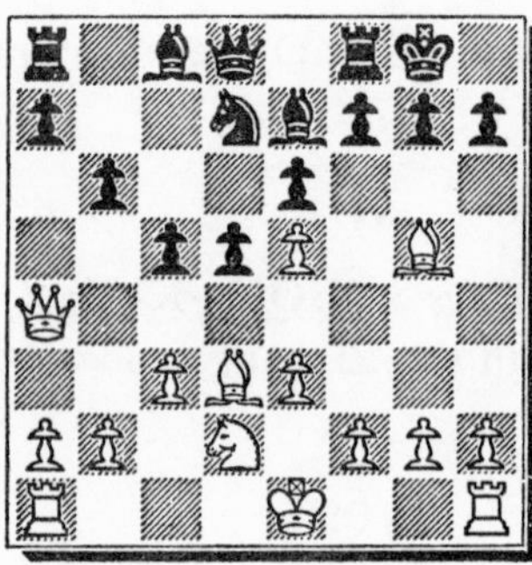

BLACK

DIAGRAM 162

WHITE *to play*

In this position most players would thoughtlessly choose *1* BxB or else *1* B–KB4.

The fact is, though, that White has a much stronger move at his disposal. What is that move?

BLACK *to play*

DIAGRAM 163

WHITE

The most significant feature of this position is that White's Rook at Queen Bishop 1 has the double duty of defending the other White Rook and the White Bishop.

How can Black turn this to his advantage?

APPENDIX

DIAGRAM **69** (*page 109*)

White looks for a forcing, violent move:

1 **QxP** mate!

DIAGRAM **70** (*page 110*)

Black can win quickly with a forcing, violent move, a *check:*

1	**Q–B8** ch!!
2 **QxQ**	**P–K7** dis ch

Another forcing, violent move – a *discovered check* which leaves White little choice.

Thus, if *3* K–R1? Black mates on the move. Or if *3* Q–B2, PxN/Q ch and mate next move.

3 **N–B2**	**PxQ/Q** ch
4 **KxQ**	**RxN** ch

And Black's overwhelming material superiority decides the issue.

DIAGRAM **71** (*page 110*)

White's Queen move must be a forcing, violent move – a *check:*

1 **Q–N7** ch!! **BxQ**

Opening up his first rank to attack.

2 **N–B6** mate!

The deadly *double check* forces *checkmate.*

DIAGRAM 72 (*page 111*)

White's first move is astounding but logical.

1 **N–B6**!! ....

This forcing, violent move is a *threat:* it forks the Black Rooks and thus threatens to win the Exchange.

1 .... **KxN**

Since the loss of the Exchange would be fatal for Black in the long run, he decides to capture the Knight.

2 **N–R5** ch!! ....

This forcing, violent check leaves Black no choice, for on 2 .... K–B4 White can choose from 3 Q–N5 mate or 3 Q–B4 mate or 3 B–R3 mate.

2 .... **PxN**
3 **Q–N5** mate

Truly magnificent attacking play.

DIAGRAM 98 (*page 146*)

In order to win, Black must resort to a forcing, violent move, a *pin:*

1 .... **R–K8**!!

This paralyzes White's Queen, preventing QxQ and threatening .... Q–N7 mate!

2 **RxR** **RxR**

White must resign, as he has no defense to the coming .... Q–N7 mate.

DIAGRAM 99 (*page 146*)

White sees a forcing, violent move: *1* N–Q7 (a *Knight fork*). If played at once, however, it would be a crass blunder, as Black would have an even more forcing, violent reply: *1* .... RxQ CHECK. Therefore:

1 **QxR** ch! ....

This forcing, violent move is a *check*.

1 .... **KxQ**
2 **N–Q7** ch ....

Now this *Knight-forking check* does the trick.

2 .... **K** moves
3 **NxQ** **NxN**

With a Rook for three Pawns, White has an easy win.

DIAGRAM 100 (*page 147*)

Black must avoid *1* .... QxP ?? which would permit the crushing reply 2 BxP ch! (*discovered attack* with *check*), winning the Black Queen.

But Black has a forcing, violent move in:

1 .... **R–N5** !

Double attack.

2 **QxBP** ....

The only way to protect his Bishop.

2 .... **B–N2**

A forcing, violent move: he threatens White's Queen, which has no escape!

DIAGRAM 101 (*page 147*)

Only a forcing, violent move can save the situation for White.

1 **R–Q7** !! ....

White attacks the Black Queen, which cannot run away; for example, *1* .... Q–B1 ??; *2* RxP ch and White mates next move.

1	**QxR**
2 **N–R6** ch!	....

Another forcing, violent move – *check* with *discovered attack* on Black's Queen.

2	**PxN**
3 **QxQ**	....

Thanks to his attack on Black's Queen Bishop, White will have time to win two Black Pawns with overwhelming material superiority.

DIAGRAM **125** (*page 178*)

White wins by means of a forcing, violent move – a *check* that stamps Black's Queen as an *overworked piece.*

1 **R–B8** ch!	**QxR**

Forced – but now Black's defense against the original mating attack has collapsed.

2 **QxNP** ch!	....

Another forcing, violent *check.*

2	**RxQ**
3 **RxR** mate	

Note that this checkmate became possible after the forced disappearance of Black's Queen from the second rank.

DIAGRAM **126** (*page 178*)

As we know, Black's Queen at King 2 is the heart of the defense. Therefore White intensifies his *threat* with a new *threat* – a forcing, violent move:

1 **B–KR4** !!	**Q–Q2**

If *1* .... QxB; 2 Q–B7 mate.

If *1* .... Q–N2 (or *1* .... QxP); 2 Q–Q8 ch!, NxQ; 3 RxN mate.

If *1* .... B–K3; 2 QxB winning a piece.

If *1* .... Q–K3; 2 Q–B5 wins.

2 **Q–B5** **P–N3**

Vain counterattack.

3 **QxN !!** ....

Another forcing, violent move – a *capture.*

3 .... **QxQ**
4 **R–Q8** mate

DIAGRAM **127** (*page 179*)

White wins by forcing, violent moves:

1 **P–N6 !** ....

This attacks Black's Queen, but above all it threatens QxP mate, therefore ruling out *1* .... QxB ?? as a reply.

1 .... **QxNP**

In the event that Black plays *1* .... PxP ?? the forcing, violent *threat* 2 N–N5 leaves Black helpless to prevent checkmate.

2 **BxN !** ....

Another forcing, violent move – a *capture.* Black has no good reply, for *2* .... QxQ; *3* BxQ leaves White a piece ahead. And on *2* .... QxB White has a forcing, violent move in *3* R–N1 (a *pin*) which wins the Black Queen.

DIAGRAM **128** (*page 179*)

As Black is being subjected to a *double attack,* he can only hope to extricate himself by an even more forcing, violent reply.

1 .... **B–Q3 !!**

This *double attack* is just the kind of forcing, violent move that Black needs. If White replies 2 R/B7xB, Black continues 2 .... BxN remaining a piece ahead.

2 **R/Q1xB** **N–K1!**

And this forcing, violent move – a *Knight fork* – is the refutation of White's plan.

With both of his Rooks attacked, White has no choice.

3 **RxB** **NxR**

After this forcing, violent move – a *capture* – Black wins easily with his advantage of the Exchange ahead.

DIAGRAM **139** (*page 193*)

From the diagram, play proceeds:

1	Q–N3
2 Castles	QxP ??

Black knows that it is bad on principle to put his Queen out of play in this fashion. But he feels that by gaining time through his attack on White's Queen Knight, he can escape unscathed.

Thus, if White continues 3 N–QR4, there follows 3 .... Q–N5 with *double attack* on White's Knight on Queen Rook 4 and White's Bishop on King Bishop 4. All very plausible, but instead White chooses a forcing, violent move:

3 **N–QN5!** ....

With the *threat* of the *Knight-forking check* N–B7 ch, winning Black's Queen Rook.

3 .... **K–Q1**

Black defends himself against the threat, but now White plays another forcing, violent move:

4 **B–Q2!** ....

With the terrible *threat* of 5 B–B3, winning Black's trapped Queen!

4 .... **P–Q5**

Preventing White's B–B3.

5 **Q–K2!** ....

Still another forcing, violent move with the *threat* of 6 KR–N1, winning the Black Queen. As the Black Queen is trapped, Black has no satisfactory defense. Thus we conclude that by playing 2 .... QxP ?? Black fell into a trap.

DIAGRAM **140** (*page 193*)

If Black tries to win a Pawn, he falls into a fatal trap:

1 .... **PxP** ??
2 **BxP** ch! ....

This forcing, violent *check* leaves Black no choice.

2 .... **KxB**

Black's King, which has the function of guarding Black's Queen, is an *overworked piece.*

3 **QxQ** ....

And White has an overwhelming material advantage.

DIAGRAM **141** (*page 194*)

In order to prevent the loss of a Pawn, Black plays:

1 .... **B–N5** ?

However, this move is ineffectual in view of the forcing, violent moves White has at his command.

2 **PxP!** ....

A forcing, violent move – a *capture.*

The point is that on 2 .... PxP White has another forcing, violent move: 3 BxP ch! (a *capture* with *check*), so that after

3 .... KxB he can play *4* NxP ch (a *capture* with *check,* plus *discovered attack* on Black's Bishop on King Knight 5). Then, after Black's King moves, White continues *5* NxB, regaining the sacrificed piece and remaining two Pawns ahead. This is a splendid example of a sequence of forcing, violent moves to achieve a specific purpose.

2 .... **NxB**

Black sees through White's plan – up to a point – and therefore removes the obnoxious Bishop.

3 **RPxN** **PxP**

True, White's King Knight remains *pinned* and consequently *4* NxP ?? is out of the question. Nevertheless, Black is still proved to be in the wrong. (Incidentally, if he had played *3* .... BxN; *4* PxB !, PxP etc., White would still have won by the text continuation.)

4 **RxP** ! ....

This forcing, violent move – a *capture* – has been overlooked by Black.

4 .... **RxR**
5 **QxP** ch ....

Another forcing, violent move: this *capture* sets up a *double attack* with *check.* White wins the Black Rook, remaining with two Pawns to the good.

DIAGRAM **142** (*page 194*)

Black is fully justified in regaining his sacrificed Pawn at once with:

1 .... **NxQBP** !!

This clever move sets up two picturesque traps.

In the first place, if White plays *2* BxN ch, then after *2* .... PxB; *3* QxB ?? will not do because of Black's forcing, violent reply *3* . . . . N–Q6 ch – a *Knight-forking check* that wins the White Queen.

2 QxB ?? **. . . .**

White tries a different way. He thinks this capture is feasible because Black's Knight at Queen Bishop 3 is pinned.

But here too Black has a forcing, violent reply.

2 . . . . **N–Q6 ch!**

At first sight this *Knight-forking check* looks nonsensical, as the Knight can be captured.

3 BxN **. . . .**

Of course. But now White has been forced to give up his *pin,* whereupon the capture of his Queen becomes operative.

3 . . . . **NxQ**

And Black has an overwhelming material advantage.

DIAGRAM **160** (*page 215*)

White's first move is obvious:

1 NxBP ! **Q–Q2**

If Black plays *1* . . . . Q–B3 or *1* . . . . Q–B2 or *1* . . . . Q–N2 instead, White still wins with the same ingenious reply.

2 N–K7 ch!! **. . . .**

This forcing, violent move – a *Knight-forking check* – leaves Black helpless. If he now moves his King, White simply continues *3* NxR, winning the Exchange.

2 . . . . **QxN**
3 QxR ! **. . . .**

The point! White is the Exchange ahead (if *3* . . . . BxQ; *4* RxQ etc.).

DIAGRAM **161** *(page 216)*

Black's winning move is:

1 .... **Q–N3 !**

This forcing, violent move *pins* White's Knight at Queen 4, which cannot move because it screens White's King from attack on the diagonal.

Since the vulnerable Knight is doubly attacked, White must bring up additional defense. But the defending piece will also be vulnerable!

2 **B–K3** **P–K4 !**

This forcing, violent move is a *threat.* Black threatens to capture the vulnerable Knight, which is unable to move because then Black captures the unprotected White Bishop at King 3 *with check.*

3 **N–R4** ....

Counterattack on the Black Queen. (Perhaps Black will foolishly give up his *threat* on the diagonal.)

3 .... **Q–R2 !**

Black maintains his threat on the diagonal.

4 **NxN** **QxB** ch

Another forcing, violent move – Black *captures* the Bishop *with check.* Consequently White must get his King out of check, allowing Black to continue *5* .... PxN with a piece ahead.

DIAGRAM **162** *(page 216)*

White's strongest move is:

1 **Q–R4 !** ....

This forcing, violent move embodies two *threats:* (a) *2* QxP mate, and (b) *2* BxB followed by *3* BxR (after Black's Queen moves), leaving White a whole Rook ahead.

If Black makes a feeble attempt to parry both threats with *1* .... P–B3 there follows *2* QxP ch, K–B2; *3* B–N6 mate.

DIAGRAM 163 (*page 217*)

Black wins by means of a forcing, violent move:

1 .... **RxB** ch!

Demonstrating that White's Rook at Queen Bishop 1 is an *overworked piece.*

2 **RxR** **QxR**

Black has won a piece.